THE
176
STUPIDEST
THINGS
EVER DONE

Also by Ross and Kathryn Petras

The 776 Stupidest Things Ever Said
The 776 Even Stupider Things Ever Said
The 776 Nastiest Things Ever Said

THE 176 STUPIDEST

Things

EVER DONE

Ross and Kathryn Petras

Main Street Books
DOUBLEDAY
New York London Toronto Sydney Auckland

A MAIN STREET BOOK
PUBLISHED BY DOUBLEDAY
a division of Bantam Doubleday Dell Publishing Group, Inc.
1540 Broadway, New York, New York 10036

MAIN STREET BOOKS, DOUBLEDAY, and the portrayal of a building
with a tree are trademarks of Doubleday,
a division of Bantam Doubleday Dell Publishing Group, Inc.

BOOK DESIGN BY CAROL MALCOLM RUSSO / SIGNET M DESIGN, INC.

Library of Congress Cataloging-in-Publication Data
Petras, Ross.
The 176 stupidest things ever done / Ross & Kathryn Petras. — 1st ed.
p.   cm.
"Main Street Books."
1. Anecdotes.   I. Petras, Kathryn.   II. Title.
PN6262.P48   1996
082—dc20   96-12538
                                                             CIP

ISBN 0-385-48341-4

Introduction

A few years ago, we put together *The 776 Stupidest Things Ever Said*—a look at the fine art of placing the foot in the mouth. And the book became a bestseller—as did its spin-off sequels and annual calendars.

But we couldn't stop there.

It got us to thinking: What about the *doers* out there? The people of action who, instead of saying something stupid, go right out and *do* something stupid?

It's time to give credit where credit is due.

So now we've collected *The 176 Stupidest Things Ever Done*—a compilation of inane incidents, senseless stunts, farcical feats, and utterly asinine activities.

These are examples of the sublimely stupid, committed by the famous and not-so-famous. It includes celebrities like Sam Goldwyn, athletes like Charles Barkley, politicians like Ronald Reagan, semi-stars like Fabio, and institutions ranging from the board of General Motors to the various agencies of the federal government. And, of course, it also includes the unsung heroes of stupidity, the average Joes and Janes who are responsible for so many inspired moments of lunacy.

Committing a stupid action isn't as simple as you might think.

Actually, it's a bit of a science. As students of stupidity, we've discovered that there are distinct types of stupid actions, including:

☞ **the Bureaucratic Bungle:** When red tape spawns red faces. The inevitable result of following the rules instead of common sense, this type of institutional inanity is committed by any large organization—from the government to schools to corporations.

☞ **the Inspired Idiocy:** Ingenuity gone insane. This is a stupid action committed by a person with creativity, vision . . . and an amazingly ridiculous idea. Favored by people who suddenly wonder just why it is that no one has ever crossed the English Channel in a motorized bathtub . . . and who have the nerve (or the insanity) to actually try it.

☞ **the Enigmatic Eccentricity:** A bit like the inspired idiocy, but more of a lifestyle. This is the specialty of people who make nonconformity into an art form—a dying breed nowadays, as mass culture spawns mass group-think. Happily, there are still enough brave individualistic souls who follow their own drummer, to whatever bizarre and silly ends it may take them.

☞ **the Asinine Alibi:** When people are caught in the act, but feel it necessary to explain anyway in a futile and ridiculous attempt to clear their name. The result? Looking guilty—and stupid—at the same time. This type of stupidity is especially prevalent in courtrooms, police stations, and anywhere politicians are found.

☞ **the Big Business Blunder:** Capitalism run amok. This occurs when business goes overboard in trying to sell a product, make a profit, or keep the wheels of commerce turning. It can be something like a global advertising mistranslation that makes people think they can prevent pregnancy by buying certain ink to a product promotion that stinks . . . literally.

☞ **the Trying-Too-Hard-Not-to-Make-a-Mistake Mishap:** Something that happens to everyone at one time or another—especially to anal-retentive perfectionists. You're trying so hard to make everything go well that it all blows up in your face.

☞ **the Bad Timing Fiasco:** Just what it sounds like. Everything is going smoothly, then the worst happens . . . at the worst possible moment. Often occurs just after someone has made a sweeping generalization like "This is the safest building ever built" right before the building collapses.

☞ **the Preposterous Production:** Stupidity onstage (or on television or on film). This is a dramatic form of stupidity in action, commonly produced by auteurs who have a unique vision ("King Lear on roller skates!") and wonder why no one else thought of it.

☞ **the Politically Correct but Dumb:** When people are so worried about being inoffensive that they wind up being idiotic instead. Practiced by governments, schools, and well-meaning types in particular, this type of stupidity proves that there is such a thing as being too concerned about what other people think.

☞ **the Simply Stupid:** Just plain stupidity, pure and simple.

As an added treat, *The 176 Stupidest Things Ever Done* includes Special Sections on specific areas of stupid actions, such as:

☞ **Government Gaffes:** A nonpartisan, nonethnocentric, all-inclusive collection of governmental nonsense that proves the public's sneaking suspicion that, if you want something done stupidly, ask the government.

☞ **Science Goes Stupid:** Proof that an advanced degree doesn't necessarily mean you've got the greatest smarts in the world. This section contains examples of the most ridiculous research imaginable.

☞ **Idiotic Inventions and Products We Could Live Without:** A rundown of utterly useless products that no one needs, but, for some reason, intrepid inventors and not-so-savvy product developers keep foisting on the public.

☞ **Stupid Songs:** Music that doesn't make you want to tap your feet, snap your fingers, or sing along, but does make you laugh. This includes lyrics and titles of some of the absolutely worst songs ever written.

☞ **Lunatic Laws:** A listing of the most ridiculous laws around—evidence that the legal system is as laughable as you might have thought.

☞ **Criminally Stupid:** Examples of extremely *im*-perfect crimes committed by less-than-brilliant criminal minds.

In short, we've made every effort to cover it all. If it's something someone did that's stupid, we've tried to include it. As you can see, *The 176 Stupidest Things Ever Done* is a celebration of all of us—and the stupid things we all do at one time or another. It salutes the buffooneries, travesties of common sense, and just plain stupid things people have done.

If you know about—or have committed yourself—something you

consider one of the stupidest things ever done, we'd love to hear about it. We're always on the lookout for more stupidities to use in our sequels. Please send us a brief description of the incident and include the date, time, and place you heard it or, if it's something you found in the papers or magazines, send us a clipping. And let us know if you want to be credited in print for your contribution. Send your "stupidest thing ever done" to:

Ross and Kathryn Petras
c/o Doubleday
1540 Broadway
New York, NY 10036

THE
176
STUPIDEST
THINGS
EVER DONE

A

ON ADVERTISING, GREAT MOMENTS IN:

Sumitomo was a giant Japanese steelmaker that developed a special super-tough steel pipe. They were sure it would be snapped up by the Americans.

It was a good product, but there was one problem. Sumitomo had hired a Japanese advertising agency instead of an American one.

The agency named the steel pipe Sumitomo High Toughness, to show up its strength. But to make it all easier to remember, the agency decided to emphasize the initials of the Sumitomo High Toughness steel pipe as a sort of shortened brand name. So, in a series of huge two-page ads in major business magazines throughout the United States, startled customers saw ads like this:

SHT—from Sumitomo
Now, Sumitomo brings SHT to the United States.

At the bottom of the ads, Sumitomo assured customers that their product "was made to match its name."

ON ADVICE, NOT FOLLOWING YOUR OWN:

Mrs. Dwight Morrow was expecting famous financier J. P. Morgan for tea—and she was a bit concerned. The problem was J. P. Morgan's nose. It was large, bright red, and altogether conspicuous. Mrs. Morrow was worried that one of her two young daughters, particularly Anne (who later became a writer and married Charles Lindbergh), might say something untoward about Morgan's nose and ruin the tea.

So she sat the two girls down before Morgan was supposed to arrive and explained to them that children sometimes saw odd or interesting things, but they didn't have to comment on them. In particular, she warned them to say nothing at all about anything about Mr. Morgan's appearance that might strike them as peculiar.

Mr. Morgan arrived and, much as Mrs. Morrow had feared, little Anne and her sister were transfixed by Morgan's nose. As discreetly as possible, she tried to hurry the girls out of the room before they forgot themselves and said something. Finally the girls curtsied and left the room—and Mrs. Morrow drew her first relaxed breath. The crisis point had passed. They could now have their tea in peace.

"And now, Mr. Morgan," she said, turning to him, "will you have one or two lumps of sugar in your nose?"

ON AGE, IMPORTANCE OF, IN HOLDUPS:

It began as a typical holdup, this time in Los Angeles in 1994. A young man came into a liquor store, waved his gun at the man behind the counter, and yelled for the clerk to give him all the money in the cash register. And the clerk, realizing this wasn't a game, quickly did as he was told.

Then the thief spotted a bottle of good Scotch on the shelf behind the clerk. He asked the clerk to hand that over as well. But this time the clerk didn't comply. "Absolutely not," he told the thief.

This wasn't in the usual script. The thief was nonplussed. "Why can't I have the Scotch?" he asked the clerk.

"You have to be twenty-one to get liquor," the clerk said—as he probably said hundreds of times a day.

"But I am twenty-one," protested the thief.

The clerk wouldn't buy it. No legal ID, no booze.

The frustrated thief finally pulled out his wallet and showed his photo driver's license to the clerk. See, he *was* legal.

Good enough. The clerk gave the bottle to the thief, who left happy.

Then the clerk called the police and gave them the name and address of the thief—who he knew would be charged as an adult.

ON AIR TRAVEL, STRANGE:

In early 1983, a man from the Los Angeles area had a great idea: Why not *fly* instead of drive to his girlfriend's house?

The logistics of how he would accomplish this were ingeniously simple. He would get a lightweight pool lounge chair. He would attach helium weather balloons all around the chair. Then he would simply sit in the chair and float upward into the sky. Besides a beer, he would bring with him a small air pistol, to shoot and pop the balloons one by one when he wanted to lose altitude or return to earth.

Simple.

On the day of the flight, things went off without a hitch . . . during the first few minutes. The balloons rose according to plan, carrying the man and his lounge chair up into the sky. As the man achieved his desired altitude, he got ready to shoot a few balloons to stabilize his altitude. He took aim . . . and then dropped the air pistol.

And now the lounge chair kept rising.

At ten thousand feet, the winds took him out near the skies of LAX—Los Angeles International Airport.

The radio tower chatter from airline pilots reported the unusual sight of a man in a lounge chair loafing in the air lanes. One pilot reported a UFO, under the somewhat logical reasoning that he couldn't be seeing a man in a lounge chair with a beer at what was now fifteen thousand feet above the earth. . . .

Finally the winds blew the man and lounge chair back toward suburbia. And as the helium slowly leaked out of the balloons, the lounge chair gradually began to descend, and then, fittingly, landed right by the side of a backyard family swimming pool.

ON ALIBIS, HAIRY:

A burglar, John Bristol, was caught red-handed on his hands and knees in an apartment. But as he told the police, he really wasn't a burglar at all. "I was passing the time between trains," he explained.

But what about the screwdriver he was holding?

"I was using it to squash a hairy bug that had attached itself to the front door."

ON ALIBIS, ROCK-SOLID:

Christine Powers, the mother of a young man accused of committing a drive-by shooting in New Orleans, was outraged. The police were clearly trying to frame her son. She was positive he was innocent.

"The facts are black-and-white," she said. "Steve couldn't possibly have been involved because, at exactly ten-thirty, when this shooting took place, he was over the other side of town in a housing project, murdering someone who owed us money."

ON ANATOMY, EXTRA-SPECIAL:

A young man who worked as a fish filleter was a finalist in the Morecambe and Heysham, England, "Sexy Boy" male beauty contest—and he was definitely making an impression on the judges and the crowd. But just as he left the stage to cheers from those watching, he was asked to step into the inspection tent by a pageant official for a closer examination. Something seemed, well, fishy.

The contestant complied. He took off his swim trunks as the official asked. It was then that the official saw why the contestant was such a crowd pleaser: Under the swimsuit, the man was wearing a jockstrap into which a power drill was stuffed.

The man claimed that it was all a terrible mistake. He had taken the drill with him for "security reasons"—"and just before my name was called, I realized it would be foolish to leave it behind in the dressing room."

ON ANCIENT COINS, EXPERTS AND:

The South Shields Museum in England was sponsoring an exhibition of Roman artifacts found nearby. Proudly displayed in one case was a vintage Roman sestertius coin. It was identified by museum experts as having been minted almost two thousand years before, somewhere around A.D. 135.

However, one visiting expert disagreed. Little Fiona Gordon, age nine, identified the coin as a plastic token given away by a local soda bottler.

Museum experts were amused, and asked her to prove this cute idea. So Fiona pointed out the soda bottler's trademark on the back of the coin.

Embarrassed museum officials started explaining. According to a spokesperson, "The token was designed as a Roman replica. The trouble was that we construed the letter 'R' on the coin to mean 'Roma.' In fact, it stood for 'Robinson's,' the soft drink manufacturers."

The museum promised to view with "great suspicion" any coins donated in the future.

ON AQUATIC CROSSINGS, FIZZLING

Mary Connor was a woman with a goal. She wanted to be the first female human cannonball to be shot across the River Avon. And, in 1972, she decided to make her dream come true.

By the banks of the river, before a large crowd, she set up her cannon. As the audience waited in anxious anticipation, Connor got into her cannon and slid down the barrel. An assistant lit the charge. There was a huge bang and the cannon fired . . . but Connor didn't shoot out. In fact, nothing happened at all.

So Connor tried again—and the second time things went a little better. The cannon fired, and Connor shot out. Unfortunately, the cannon went off at a half charge—so Connor only made it halfway, landing with a large splash in the middle of the river.

But, following the old adage "If at first you don't succeed . . . ," Connor climbed out of the water to try one more time. Still dripping wet from round two, the dauntless woman arrived at the cannon for a third try, this time sporting a bandaged ankle and bandaged elbows. As she explained to curious onlookers, she had scraped them last time she shot out of the cannon.

Now again, Connor clambered into the cannon barrel and waited for it to be fired.

The assistant lit the charge, the cannon roared—and this time Connor soared up and out—higher and higher. But as the audience could see, this time she shot out ass-backward, and not only landed in the river again, but managed to hit a rescue boat waiting for any accident. She capsized it, and together with the crew, swam back to shore.

ON ARRESTS:

Alert police in Cumbria, England, arrested a man for public drunkenness because of his "glazed expression." He was released when he appeared in court and showed the judge his glass eye.

ON AUTOBIOGRAPHIES:

Charles Barkley, the famous outspoken basketball player, was furious.

He had been badly, badly misquoted in a book about his life and career, titled *Outrageous*. There was one thing to do. The outraged basketball player immediately tried to stop the publishers from putting out the offending book.

There was one little problem. The book *Outrageous* was Barkley's own book—his autobiography.

(Apparently, Barkley relied on his "coauthor," Roy Johnson, to read the galleys of the book. *The New Republic* called him one of the first authors to "fail to read a book before he failed to write it.")

B

On Bank Robbers, Farsighted:

It was a lot like a scene from a gangster movie: Two masked men rushed into a bank (it happened to be in Jaumpur in the Indian state of Uttar Pradesh), guns drawn, and demanded that the manager behind the counter hand over the money—pronto.

Although the guns were very convincing, the manager hesitated. He didn't have any money, he explained.

"Impossible. Isn't this a bank?" one of the robbers asked.

"Yes. An eye bank."

There is a happy ending, though. The manager wound up convincing the robbers to pledge their eyes.

On Bank Robbers, Revolving:

Three men decided to rob the Royal Bank of Scotland in 1975. But they got off on the wrong foot—and never recovered.

It all started when they got stuck in the revolving doors of the bank entrance. The incompetent criminals were finally freed by the bank staff, and they left the building.

They reappeared a few minutes later and announced they were

robbing the bank. But the reaction wasn't what they expected. Everyone burst into laughter. Everyone thought it was a wonderful practical joke.

The robbers persisted. First they asked for £5,000, but the cashier was laughing so hard that he didn't give it to them. The desperate robbers reduced their demand to £500, then £50. Finally they asked for anything, just *anything*. But to no avail.

Finally, in desperation, one of the trio vaulted over the counter to get the money. But instead he tripped and landed on his ankle, badly spraining it. The other two now decided to make their getaway. They got as far as the revolving door . . . where they got stuck again.

ON BASERUNNING, CONFUSING MOMENTS IN:

On April 17, 1993, the Baltimore Orioles were playing the California Angels—and wound up getting cited by *Sports Illustrated* for making the stupidest play of the year.

The Orioles had the bases loaded and only one man out. Oriole Mike Devereaux was up. The second he hit the ball, the runner at third, Jeff Tackett, headed for home. But Devereaux's line drive wasn't deep enough. The ball was caught by the Angel center fielder.

Keeping his cool, Tackett headed back to third. But when he got there, he also found Brady Anderson, the runner from second, on the bag—and Chito Martinez, the runner from first, as well.

California catcher John Orton tagged all three—and two were called out for an inning-ending double play.

The California third baseman summed it up: "It wouldn't have been the stupidest play until Chito arrived at third. I think he thought there was a fight, so he ran across the field to get in it."

ON BASKETBALL COACHES, NOT-SO-INSPIRING:

If you want to lose basketball games, you might want a coach like the Friendsville Academy Foxes basketball team had.

From 1967 to 1973, the team chalked up 128 consecutive losses. They lost one game 71 to 0. They came closest to victory once when they lost 2 to 0—but the winning basket was scored by a Friendsville player who erroneously shot the ball into the wrong hoop. The coach decided not to give pep talks because he believed they made his players nervous.

But if there is any doubt that this coach deserves special mention, the clincher comes in 1970. That year the coach named one player—a player who had never scored a single point—the team's most outstanding player. When reporter Douglas S. Looney from the *National*

Observer questioned the coach, the coach had a succinct reply: "You don't think scoring is everything, do you?"

The absurd conversation continued.

"Is there anything this team does well?" asked the reporter.

"Not really," replied the coach.

"Are you making any progress?"

"I couldn't truthfully say that we are."

"Do you like coaching?"

"I don't care that much for basketball."

ON BEAR RESCUES, WHEN TO BAG:

A black bear was stuck in a pine tree in Keithville, Louisiana. And everyone wanted to help rescue it.

People began gathering under the tree, peering up at the large bear and trying to help lure it down. But even the efforts of the game warden and a veterinarian armed with tranquilizing darts failed.

They had been trying for about eight hours, when the local sheriff was called. About eight hundred people were gathered under the tree, and the sheriff was needed to control the huge mob.

When he arrived, though, his presence wasn't needed anymore. The eight hundred people were beginning to disperse. The rescue effort had succeeded.

They had managed to rescue the large black garbage bag that had gotten caught in the tree.

ON BEE-AVOIDANCE MOVES:

A man was fishing in the Amazon's Rio Negro when his line got stuck in a tree. He began pulling and tugging at the line to free it, when the line hit a bees' nest. The infuriated bees went for him. He swatted, jumped, ran, but the bees kept attacking. Desperate to get away, he finally leaped into the river.

He was promptly eaten by piranhas.

ON BIOTECH BREAKTHROUGHS, GREAT RUSSIAN MOMENTS IN:

In the mid-1980s, Soviet scientists announced a breakthrough in animal breeding—an amphibious chicken.

As they explained to the official communist news agency, TASS, these chickens "leap fearlessly into pools and pick grains from the depths. . . . Members from the Central Committee gazed with astonishment when they saw Lupha, our Siberian blue spat chicken, throw itself into the water tank and go to sleep on the bottom."

The tireless Soviet scientists announced that they weren't stopping with underwater chickens. They said they were also hoping to work on amphibious mice, amphibious cats, and one day, maybe even amphibious monkeys.

ON BIRDWATCHERS, OVERLY DEVOTED:

A devoted birdwatcher decided that the only way to band the swans living on a nearby lake in upstate New York was to disguise himself.

A conscientious fellow, he decided to do things properly. He decided to approach the swans—as a swan. So he put the hollowed-out and dried body of a swan over his head and waded out onto the lake.

Unfortunately, it was midnight, he couldn't swim, and he drowned.

ON BLACKMAIL, BAD SETUPS:

A man with a beautiful girlfriend had a perfect plan for raising cash. He would find a rich married lawyer, she would seduce him, and together they would blackmail the sucker!

It couldn't fail.

So, one night, while his girlfriend accomplice attracted the right rich lawyer, the man hid in her hotel room closet with a flash camera ready.

Soon the girlfriend brought the lawyer into the room, and not long afterward, lovemaking began.

Steady, now! The man waited for just the right moment. Then—*snap!*—the picture was taken and the man triumphantly burst open the closet and demanded blackmail money from the lawyer.

All seemed fine until the lawyer looked at the picture—it was a wonderful shot of the refrigerator in the corner of the room.

ON BOOKSTORES:

Whenever anyone says that the literacy rate isn't declining, consider this story from a woman who recently went to a bookstore to find a copy of *Mein Kampf*.

The bookseller asked: "Is that the author?"

The woman answered: "No, it's German for *My Struggle*. It's by Hitler."

The bookseller: "Hitler who?"

The woman: "Are you serious?"

The bookseller (raising eyes in pained look): "Look. I don't know *every* author in the world."

On Boxing Techniques, Overdoing:

It was an important bout for boxer Danny Osnato—and his trainer told him exactly how to play it. His advice: Dance the first round out. If Osnato kept dancing, the other guy wouldn't be able to lay a glove on him. Then, in the second round, Osnato should start swinging.

The obedient boxer did just what his trainer said. And it worked. Osnato's footwork was phenomenal. The opponent didn't hit him once.

But after forty-seven seconds of intense dancing, Osnato dropped to the canvas, unconscious.

His opponent won on a TKO.

On Bullfights:

Spain has always loved bullfights.

But when the country was under the rule of Generalissimo Francisco Franco, the Nazi-loving fascists decided that sticking and killing bulls just wasn't brutal enough.

So they decided to enliven things a bit. They took a bull, and for an added touch, put a tiger into the ring.

The fascist crowd at the bullfight went wild with excitement. A *bull and tiger* fight!

But the tiger was a gentle sort. Instead of ripping the bull apart, he sat down in the middle of the ring, next to the bull, and started licking it.

This love fest continued for some time. The crowd got angrier and angrier. Soon furious fascists were booing, then more lively ones began throwing things at the happy couple. Finally a mob jumped into the ring and started kicking the lackadaisical bull and tiger. The bull and tiger didn't like this and started getting aggressive—against the crowd.

And that's when General Franco's elite fascist military police decided to take things in hand. Firing machine guns, they entered the ring. They somehow missed the tiger and only wounded the bull, but they did manage to machine-gun and kill seventeen overexcited spectators.

ON BUREAUCRACY, GREAT MOMENTS IN, ELEVATOR:

Q: Why did the three New Jersey towns of Upper Pittsgrove, Alloway, and Quinton each hire an elevator inspector when there were absolutely no elevators in any building in any of the towns?

A: Because the state government told them to.

With impeccable bureaucratic logic, the New Jersey Department of Consumer Affairs explained that by law all 567 towns in New Jersey are required to have elevator inspectors.

Even if the town doesn't have an elevator?

No exceptions, a brilliant bureaucratic spokesperson explained. "Otherwise, the Uniform Construction Code would no longer be uniform."

ON BURGLARY METHODS, INDISCREET:

The key to burglary is to pick your target well.

This was where a burglar in Longmont, Colorado, went wrong. All was going well at the store he was attempting to rob. He was busy prying open the front door with a crowbar. Then he stopped. Something seemed a little wrong. . . .

He looked up. A large number of people were *inside* the store. And they were staring at him.

At this moment, the master burglar realized that the store was still open.

C

On Calling 911, Stupid Reasons for:

Thank *The Los Angeles Times* for this eye-opening list of calls California 911 operators have gotten:

- Eighteen-year-old male couldn't get any rest at home and wanted a ride to the hospital.
- Thirteen-year-old stubbed her toe on a stereo speaker.
- Lady got blisters from working three days at a Taco Bell.
- Man was out of breath from running from the police.
- Person answered no to the question: "Are you conscious?"

On Campaign Advertising:

It was election time in Ecuador. And a company that put out a foot deodorant called Pulvapies decided to tie in their advertising campaign with the upcoming municipal elections. They came up with a clever slogan: "Vote for any candidate, but if you want well-being and hygiene, vote for Pulvapies."

Then came phase two of the ad campaign, an equally ingenious tie-in: On election eve, the company rolled out nationwide distribution of a leaflet designed to look just like a ballot. The leaflet read: FOR MAYOR: HONORABLE PULVAPIES.

The campaign was effective—but not in the way the company had planned. Yes, Pulvapies increased sales. It also got votes across the county, as befuddled voters marked their ballots for the Honorable Pulvapies—and, by a definitive majority, the footpowder was elected mayor of the small coastal town of Picoaza.

On Campaigns, Stupid Moments In:

Dan Quayle, extending his hand during a campaign stop at Hardee's: "I'm Dan Quayle. Who are you?"

Woman: "I'm your Secret Service agent."

On Car Testing, Stupid Moves In:

LaVerie Williams of Beaumont, Texas, was thrilled with her new car and wanted to test every aspect of it—including the capacity of the car's trunk. So she had family members shut her inside the trunk.

That's when she realized she had the keys clutched in her hand.

ON CARMEN, UNCOMMON PRODUCTION OF:

Opera fans in Heidelberg, Germany, were watching a first-class production of the opera *Carmen,* conducted by Ian Reid. At last, the moment the audience had been waiting for—the climactic scene when Don Jose stabs Carmen in the heart with his knife.

Unfortunately, when the actor playing Don Jose approached Carmen for the fatal stab, he realized something horrible. He had forgotten his toy knife! Still singing away lustily, Don Jose thought quickly. He would pretend to strangle Carmen instead.

He proceeded to put his hands around Carmen's neck. But the woman playing Carmen didn't know Don Jose had forgotten his toy knife. . . .

She thought he had gone insane. She fought back fiercely, struggling to break herself free. It made for exciting theater. And in theater's best traditions, even as she thought her end was near, the woman playing Carmen kept right on singing—although the critics all agreed that her voice was a bit muffled.

ON "CAUGHT IN THE ACT" EXPLANATIONS:

Before Hugh Grant, there was TV newsman Harry Trout of Baltimore, who was acquitted of a charge of soliciting prostitutes. He explained that when saying he "wanted head" he meant he wanted to "get inside the head" of the prostitute to do a news story.

In a similar situation, an Italian priest caught nude in a whorehouse with a similarly attired thirty-two-year-old explained that he "needed this experience to understand the problems of my parishioners."

Another cleric, the not-so-Reverend Christopher Power, got off by explaining that by "oral action" he meant he wanted to "talk" to a prostitute because he understood her to be ill.

And in England, a certain Father Stephens was recognized by parishioners as having gone into sex shops a number of times. But as he explained in *The Times,* he wasn't as much repentant as angry. After all, "Different people have different releases. . . . But I have been ripped off. I spent seventy pounds on the tapes, but one of them was a blank all the way through."

ON CHARACTER ASSESSMENT:

The parishioners of a Baptist church in Illinois didn't know what they were getting when Charles Lewis first became a pastor. All they did know was that he had what is politely called "a bad past."

But during his first address to the people of the church, he decided it was the right moment to make a completely clean breast of it. From the pulpit, he revealed the horrible truth about his past: He was a reformed Mafia hit man who had killed twenty-eight people over fifteen years while working for Murder Incorporated—but while on Death Row, he found God and became reformed. That wasn't all, though. Even after his reformation, he wasn't completely clean. He had been one of the committee that planned the entire Watergate conspiracy.

The church leaders and worshippers were impressed by his willingness to be completely frank. They decided to let bygones be bygones.

But then the church got a shock about Pastor Lewis: None of his confessed sins had ever taken place.

"When the local police revealed that these incidents had never taken place—although he had strangled his second wife in 1987," said church leader Dr. Donald Morley, "we decided that he was not the man we thought he was."

ON CLEANING ELEVATORS, UPS AND DOWNS IN:

A janitor at the Marriott Hotel in Bristol, England, was asked to clean an elevator. The job took him four full days.

His confused supervisor asked him why it had taken so long. Replied the janitor, "Well, there are twelve of them, one on each floor, and sometimes some of them aren't there."

Apparently, the man had thought that each floor had a different elevator—so he went to each floor and cleaned the same elevator twelve separate times.

ON COCKROACHES, DRUG-USING:

Half a ton of marijuana, cocaine, and amphetamines, seized from drug busts, disappeared from the headquarters of the Manila, Philippines, police headquarters in 1993.

What happened?

According to the Manila police chief, the problem was obvious: The room used to store the drugs had been built badly, with a lot of cracks in the wall.

With a straight face, the chief told reporters that "Rats and cockroaches got in through gaps in the locker doors and ate it all, every last scrap."

As proof that little bugs were the culprits, he offered this observation: "We know this to be a fact, because the cockroaches at police headquarters have been behaving very oddly. They just stand there looking dazed when we shine a light on them. . . ."

When a reporter showed the chief photographs of the police selling drugs and suggested that corrupt cops were stealing them, the police chief called the reporter "filth of the earth" and added, "No one will believe your absurd allegations."

On Communist Celebrations, Graphic:

In the old days, May Day, the international socialist and communist holiday, was held with much fanfare in Moscow's Red Square. Huge banners bearing the verbose sentiments of the communists dominated the square, with slogans like LONG LIVE THE HEROIC PROLETARIAN STRUGGLE. . . .

Times have changed. Last year, a motley group of communists demonstrated under the more terse banner: CAPITALISM IS SHIT.

ON COMMUTER AIRLINES, ONES TO AVOID:

James Williams of Toronto, Ontario, boarded a plane for a commuter flight from Boston. As the only passenger, he happily settled into his seat, prepared for a quiet, short flight.

It didn't happen that way.

Ten minutes after takeoff, a loud explosion blasted from the flight deck. A blue flame flashed through the passenger cabin.

Williams started to get quite concerned.

Then the pilot suddenly appeared in the doorway to the cockpit and announced, "Pray to whichever God you hold most dear!"

He disappeared just as suddenly, apparently going back to fly the plane, because the plane landed safely fifteen minutes later.

Williams summed up the rest of his experience: "There was no explanation of any kind, and when I got into the terminal, I found my luggage had been lost on the flight."

ON COMPOSERS, DEADBEAT:

The Hong Kong tax authorities are tough. They're always on the prowl for tax evaders, particularly foreign singers and entertainers who give performances and then skip off without paying tax.

In 1984, the Hong Kong Philharmonic Society received a strongly worded letter from these tough tax men. The letter came right to the point: There was no report of tax payment from an individual who they knew was connected to the Philharmonic.

The person in question was a certain J. S. Bach, who, according to their records, had recently put on one of his concerts.

On Concerts, Explosive:

The new conductor of the Atlanta Symphony back in 1974 wanted to celebrate his appointment by adding a little zip to the performance of the *1812 Overture*.

So he put sixteen minicannons throughout the auditorium. They were to be fired electronically, one by one, during the middle and the climactic end of the overture.

As the orchestra reached the middle of the overture, the conductor pressed the button for cannon number one.

Unfortunately, it didn't work out as planned. With a roar, all sixteen cannons fired at the same time. The audience of fifteen thousand was stunned. The booming of the cannons was followed by billows of cannon smoke filling the room, choking many in the audience. But it wasn't over yet. Now the wonderful Smell-All-Tell-All Customer Safety System started sounding and spraying, drenching everyone in special antiburn foam. Despite the smoke and foam, some dazed audience members managed to make it to what they thought was safety in the foyer—only to be trampled by charging firemen with masks shouting "Geronimo!" as they rushed inside.

"I have to admit to a number of incidents," said the fire chief. "The fighters were wearing a new model of smoke mask and some of them could not see."

ON CONTESTS, DECISIVE:

The question of who owned a certain sago palm tree in Haruku, Indonesia, was the cause of a dispute between two men, a certain Mr. Djambi and a Mr. Hasnuddin.

Rather than fight or go to court, they decided to go back to traditional Indonesian ways and have a little contest. The winner would get the palm tree.

The contest rules were simple: Whoever could hold his breath underwater the longest would win. Watched by their fellow villagers, Mr. Djambi and Mr. Hasnuddin weighted themselves down with stones, took two deep breaths, jumped into the water, and then held their breaths.

Unfortunately, it was a tie . . . they both drowned.

On Counterfeiting:

A convenience store clerk in Abilene, Texas, was passed a counterfeit $100 bill—and accepted it without question . . . even though it was a foot long and five inches wide.

On Crime, Equal-Opportunity:

For some reason, a blind man in Dallas decided to steal a television set. During the burglary, all seemed to be going well.

But the blind man's getaway left a little to be desired. A neighbor spotted him when he walked into a tree.

On Crime Hauls, the Bottom Line:

Mark Mueller was possibly one of the only thieves to beg the officer who arrested him to book him on manslaughter charges instead of theft.

It all happened when the sensitive thief was caught red-handed outside of the Globe Freezer Company offices in Colorado. A special investigator spotted him and asked to see the bag he was carrying.

The investigator looked inside the bag and started laughing. When he stopped, he said, "Do you know what's in here?"

Mueller first said he wasn't sure about the meaning of the word "here."

Then the officer told him what was inside the plastic sack he had stolen: 1,800 beef rectums.

"When I told him the sack contained beef assholes," the investigator told the *Rocky Mountain News,* "he burst into tears and asked me to book him on a manslaughter charge. Otherwise, he said, he would be the butt of cruel jokes while in prison."

ON CRIME PREVENTION:

A Western businessman living in Japan had been warned about notorious pickpockets in the Tokyo subways. These notorious thieves operated during the crowded rush hour. They had a habit of grabbing wallets just as subway doors were closing, leaving the victim stuck on the train while they made off with the loot.

One morning the Western businessman was at his usual subway stop when the train pulled in. He boarded, and sure enough, just as the train doors were about to close, he felt a man rub against him.

In a panic, the Western businessman reached for his wallet. It was gone! He looked up as the doors began to close and saw that the man who had rubbed against him had now stepped off the train. And the man was looking at him with what can only be described as a victorious sneer.

Thinking fast, the businessman reached his hands between the closing train doors and grabbed the sneering thief's suit lapels. The doors closed, with the thief still on the platform, but with his lapels trapped between the doors in the tight grip of the businessman.

And now, as the train began to pull away, the expression on the thief's face changed. He began screaming as he ran along the platform with the train. Finally, halfway along the platform, the panicky thief grabbed a stanchion and his lapels tore away. As the train entered the tunnel, the businessman thought that at least he had gotten something back for his loss.

When he reached his office, he called his wife to get his credit card numbers so he could cancel them. "But, honey," she said, "I've been waiting to call you. You left your wallet on the dressing table when you went to work today."

ON CRIME, VEGETABLE:

According to Mr. Ted Varey, a local senior citizen, the crime was so horrible that it gave his wife an attack of the shingles. Coming back to their car from the supermarket, they found two coconuts and a huge cucumber arranged in a suggestive manner on the car hood.

This was the last in a series of obscene fruit-and-vegetable displays that tormented the small town of Belper, England, in 1993. The unknown criminal, known to the police as General Gherkin, had been terrorizing the community for months, ramming turnips suggestively into car exhausts and arranging fruits and vegetables on car tops in ways calculated to shock the good citizens of Belper.

But, according to officials, this last crime was the worst. "Usually, it's just an apple, an orange, and a banana," said an official knowledgeable with the case. "But now the General's started to get nasty. That last cucumber was over a foot long."

According to the *Belper Express,* the culprit is still at large, although local greengrocers are suspected.

ON CRIMINALS, GULLIBLE:

Police needed a confession from a not-too-bright criminal in Radnor, Pennsylvania. Unfortunately, the station didn't have a lie detector, so the police decided to improvise.

They put the criminal's head in a metal colander and attached wires from the colander to a copier machine. Meanwhile, they put a piece of paper in the copier that said: HE'S LYING. Every time the criminal denied his role in the crime, the cops pressed the COPY button and the message HE'S LYING came out of the machine.

Seeing this high-tech example of a modern police force working so inexorably well, the criminal confessed.

ON CROWD-PLEASING EXPOSURES, BOXERS AND:

Featherweight boxer Richard Procter was raring to go. He jumped into the ring at the World Sporting Club in London, threw his robe in the corner, and raised his gloves in the air.

He was thrilled at the incredible reception he got from the crowd—wild cheers, whistles, applause.

It was then that he realized he had forgotten to put his shorts on.

ON CUSTOMERS, SUREFIRE WAYS TO ATTRACT:

It was a fact: The Heavenly Moon restaurant in Beijing, China, served bad food.

According to the public health officer, the squid with oyster sauce "was the worst I have eaten in thirty-seven years of public service." Other customers thought the same thing—the meat was tough, the oils were rancid, the food was greasy. Which is what made the restaurant's popularity so odd. . . .

As one customer noted, "I always left the Heavenly Moon telling them their food tasted like dog dirt. Yet somehow I always went back the next day." A lot of other people were doing the same thing. In spite of the horrible food, on most days, long lines formed outside the Heavenly Moon hours before it opened.

Just what was the Heavenly Moon's secret?

Public health investigators began looking into this. They learned that the restaurant had started getting popular a few months back, after someone had thrown a dinner out the window in anger at its absolute awfulness. Apparently, the owner had retired to the kitchen for some thinking. The sauce! That was it. He would spice up the food by adding a special seasoning sauce to all the dishes!

And it worked. Most customers found the sauce a bit greasy, but they all found it strangely compelling. . . .

The lines got longer and longer. Even the investigators themselves started frequenting the restaurant, using their influence to book space weeks ahead.

When police finally moved in, they discovered the special sauce indeed had one very compelling ingredient. Pure opium paste.

In his defense, the restaurateur said, "They do it in all the restaurants in America."

S P E C I A L   S E C T I O N

CRIMINALLY STUPID

"Crime does not pay." This used to be the message in every movie and every comic book in the land. Times have changed, of course, and nowadays crime often does pay, as any half-second watching the TV news can tell you.

So maybe that's why this collection of criminally stupid capers is so refreshing, so recherché. It harkens back to a simpler time, when the criminal always got caught. And it warms the cockles of the heart of any scared suburbanite with a new alarm system and triple locks—a lot of criminals out there are truly, wonderfully incompetent. Maybe there isn't so much to be afraid of, after all.

☞ A Houston armed robber was finally caught after eight holdups in three months. What broke the case? He kept on robbing the same U-Totem store, he never bothered wearing a mask . . . and he kept holding up the same sales clerk.

☞ Another Houston robber wound up wounding himself during a robbery. He was holding up a convenience store with a knife. When he leaned over the counter to take the money from the open cash register, he stabbed himself. He apparently had forgotten to turn his knife downward.

☞ A bank robber was holding up a Portland, Oregon, bank. He didn't want to attract attention to himself, so instead of yelling out orders to the teller, he quickly scribbled them on a piece of paper and waited for the teller to reply. First, he wrote: "This is a holdup and I've got a gun" and held it up for the teller to read. The teller silently nodded. Then the robber wrote: "Put all your money in a paper bag" and shoved the note through the window. The teller frowned, then wrote his own reply: "I don't have a paper bag" and returned the note to the robber. The robber was completely befuddled. This wasn't what he had pictured happening. He took the note and left.

☞ A Detroit bank robber passed a note to a bank teller—and it said the standard thing: He was armed and the teller was to fill a bag with cash. But then the robber broke from tradition. Noticing all the video surveillance cameras around the bank and hesitant to be photographed too much, he told the teller he'd wait outside for the cash. "Just bring it out when you've got it ready." He went outside—and the police, called by the teller the second he left, caught him there, patiently waiting.

☞ A Jacksonville, Florida, robber couldn't quite get it together when it came to disguising himself. He stuck up a grocery store, wearing a paper bag with cut-out eyeholes over his head. But during the attempted stickup, the bag shifted and the eyeholes were no longer over his eyes, so he couldn't see a thing. To make matters worse, a few seconds later the bag split open, completely revealing his face to the sales clerk. She immediately recognized him as a regular customer—and called the cops when he left.

☞ According to the Hartford *Courant,* a burglar had finished robbing an apartment in Connecticut and decided that, instead of lugging his loot home on foot, he'd have a cab pick him up. So he called a taxi. It didn't come in the promised time, so he called again. Still no cab. He called twice more—but the police, alerted of an intruder in the apartment by a neighbor, came before the cab arrived. The burglar's only comment? "I'm never going to use that company again," he complained.

☞ It looked like a typical bank robbery: Two men ran into a Los Angeles bank, brandishing shotguns. "Everyone lie down on the floor!" yelled one of them. His tone—and the shotguns—convinced everyone that they had better do what he said. And that's what everyone did—tellers, security guards, customers all immediately fell to the floor. In fact, everyone was so obedient that there was no one left standing to get the robbers the money. The two robbers stood there confused for a second, then ran away.

☞ In 1978, a Danish bank robber ran out of the bank he had just robbed, clutching the money. He had no getaway car waiting, but had counted on finding a cab on the busy street. And he wasn't disappointed. He immediately saw a car with a light on a roof, flagged it down, and leaped into the backseat, shouting out his address and telling the driver to step on it. But in his haste, he didn't realize one thing: It wasn't a cab he flagged down, but a police car.

☞ Frank Gort, a San Antonio burglar, was caught and convicted. When it came time for sentencing, the judge gave him seven years. Gort was very upset—and begged the judge not to sentence him to seven years because seven was his unlucky number. The understanding judge complied. He gave him eight years.

☞ An accused purse snatcher was on trial in Tulsa, Oklahoma. Instead of going with the court-appointed defense lawyer, the thief decided he could defend himself better. So, even though he had no legal experience, he served as his own counsel. And everything went beautifully. He presented his case, seemed calm, cool, and collected—even during his cross-examination of the woman whose purse he was accused of taking—and was beginning to think he'd get off. Finally he zeroed in for his final question: "Did you get a good look at my face when I took your purse?" He got ten years.

☞ A man named George Walsh of Blandford, England, was arrested and charged with drunken driving. When he was asked for his name (and ID to back it up), he had a little explaining to do. On his driver's license, he was listed as Welsh. On his insurance, as Wilsh. On his automobile club membership, as Wulsh. And on an envelope he happened to have in his pocket, as Wlesh. All this because, he said, he was wanted by the IRA and so wanted to disguise his identity. He was ultimately charged under his *real* name: Fred Miller.

☞ A man from Texas City, Texas, was dragging a newspaper vending machine toward his still-running vehicle when he was spotted by the police. As the police officers got near, the man stopped and began reading the paper inside. He explained to the police officers that he had dragged the machine over so he could read the paper better. When one of the officers pointed out that the light was brighter where the vending machine had originally been, the man said, "I read better in the dark."

☞ Two Michigan robbers charged into a Detroit music store, waving their guns. "Nobody move!" one of the robbers ordered. The second robber then moved—and the first shot him in the head.

D

ON DEBATES, GREAT MOMENTS IN:

The Oxford debating society is known for its erudite debaters and its high level of scholarship. So when English historian Philip Guedalla was the young president of the Oxford debating society, he was very eager to show what a hot debater he was.

Guedalla came up with a great way of sounding particularly bright and witty. Before a debate, there are open questions from the audience. He asked a friend to ask him two specific questions, for which he had prepared sharp answers. The friend agreed.

The night of the debate the friend in the audience asked the first question. Guedalla came back with his witty and learned reply. The audience howled with laughter. He was just *so* witty!

Guedalla's answer to the second question was even more brilliant. The entire audience broke into spontaneous applause. Guedalla was ecstatic. This little trick was earning him a big reputation! When the applause ended, the friend stood up once more.

"What was the third question you wanted me to ask you?"

ON DEFENDANTS, OVERLY HELPFUL:

Two men were on trial in San Diego, accused of armed robbery. An eyewitness was on the stand being questioned by the prosecutor, who was taking the witness step-by-step through the incident.

"Were you at the scene when the robbery took place?" asked the prosecutor.

"Yes."

"Did you see a vehicle leave in a rush?"

Again the witness replied yes.

"Did you observe the occupants of the vehicle?"

"Yes. There were two men in the car."

Perfect. The prosecutor moved in for the kill. "Are those two men present in court today?"

At that, the two defendants helpfully raised their hands.

ON DEFENSE, HONESTY IN:

An Oklahoma man was charged with armed robbery of a store—and decided to represent himself in court. All went smoothly, until the store manager took the stand.

"Can you identify the man who held up your store?" she was asked.

"Yes. That's him," she said, pointing to the defendant. The defendant leaped to his feet and accused her of lying. "I should have blown your f——ing head off!" he shouted.

A quick pause, then he added, "If I'd been the one that was there."

ON DEMOLITIONS, DUMB:

In Pompano Beach, Florida, a retired security guard and her husband were having their usual quiet day. They had just begun to eat a light snack in front of the TV, when suddenly they heard loud noises outside—and then their house began to shake.

Someone was demolishing their house.

They leaped up. The husband tried to open the front door, but found it completely blocked by a bulldozer. His wife was luckier—she managed to get out a side window. Once outside, she confronted the man in charge, the assistant building director, and asked him what was going on. He replied by asking what had happened to the demolition order his department had sent them three months before.

Before she had a chance to tell him there had been some mistake, the bulldozer had plowed through the side of the house.

At this point, the husband ran outside and confronted the building department official. Finally the official realized there had been a bit of a slipup and stopped his demolition crew.

"Okay, it's a bit messy," he breezily said. "But since we've only removed one load-bearing wall, you don't have that much to complain about. A coat of paint and it will be as good as new."

As the woman later said to a newspaper reporter, "It was then that we attacked him."

On Diplomacy, Great Moments in:

Luxembourg is a tiny country in Europe. It's so small, it decided it didn't need to attend the European Security Conference in Helsinki. Instead, it asked the Dutch representative to look after its interests.

The Dutch representative took the job of representing both countries conscientiously, maybe a little too conscientiously. . . .

When the debate over how the conference was going to be paid for began, the Dutch diplomat ran around the conference table to the place marked LUXEMBOURG and said, in French, that the United Nations should pay.

Then the Dutch diplomat got back up and ran quickly over to the seat marked NETHERLANDS and said, in English, that each nation should pay separately.

On Divorce Court, Great Moments in:

A man was being sued for divorce on the grounds of infidelity. Appearing before a London divorce court, he was asked to explain what he and his alleged lover were doing in the bedroom in the dark.

"Playing snooker," he said.

The judge then asked him about the passionate noises the wife heard coming from the bedroom. The man was unfazed.

"Those noises were completely innocent," he assured the court. They were actually "an expression of surprise or disappointment made when playing a difficult shot."

But why was the woman nude? Because she was "doing some sewing and altering her slacks."

The divorce was granted.

On Driving Techniques:

A man in Portland, Maine, was arrested for driving a Thunderbird with a TV set welded to the hood. Apparently, he watched the program on TV with one eye and the road with the other.

Not to worry, the man said. He was a split-screen artist.

ON DRIVING TESTS, PART 1:

In West London, a man was taking a driving test to get his license to drive his motor scooter. At the test center, he was given the instructions they always gave out: He was supposed to drive on a specific route. To determine his driving skill, he would be observed by a hidden examiner. And, at some point during the drive, this examiner would suddenly appear and step in front of the scooter. This would test his braking reaction.

Easy enough. The man dutifully followed the instructions, driving carefully through the route. But when he reached the end of it, the examiner hadn't appeared in front of the scooter. So the man drove through the route another time. Then another. Still no examiner.

Finally the man pulled up to the test center and asked what was going on. He had driven through the route three times and hadn't seen the examiner. Where was he?

"We're sorry," he was told. "He stepped in front of the wrong scooter."

ON DRIVING TESTS, PART 2:

Mrs. Martha Harper ended her fifth driving test in the middle of the River Wey in Surrey, England.

Passersby saw her sitting on top of her car as it floated down the river. And, along with her, on the top of the floating car, was her very nervous driving test examiner. Fortunately, both were spotted by a passing motorboat driver and rescued.

The plucky Mrs. Harper explained what had happened.

"This was my fifth test and it had been going much better than the previous four. I'd just gone round the corner in first gear. . . . I said to myself, 'I'm too close to the edge,' and then I must have put my foot on the accelerator rather than the brake because I went straight through the railings into the river."

The driving examiner was sent home in a state of shock. But, very properly, he had managed to save his clipboard and briefcase containing Mrs. Harper's test results.

"So did she fail the test?" reporters asked. The answer from the extremely conscientious officials: "As this was a terminated test, we cannot say whether the lady passed or failed until the examiner makes his report."

ON DRIVING TESTS, PART 3:

Laura Dunne of New Braunfels, Texas, needed to renew her driver's license. Unfortunately, while driving over to get this simple task done, she suddenly realized she couldn't stop her car—and crashed through the wall of the Department of Public Safety office.

On Drug-Sniffing Dogs:

Bill Wyman of the Rolling Stones had been in the United States, but he was now returning to London. Hearing about Wyman's upcoming trip, a friend from another band gave Wyman a package and asked him to take it to London. It was for his wife, the friend explained.

Without giving it a thought, Wyman tossed the package in his suitcase and forgot about it—until he disembarked at Heathrow Airport and went to pick up his baggage.

Dogs specially trained to scent out contraband, particularly drugs, were surveying all the incoming luggage. When they got to Wyman's suitcase, they went crazy. Customs officials immediately seized Wyman for questioning.

A panicking Wyman assumed his friend had set him up and immediately began explaining to the customs officials that he had no idea what was in the bag. He was delivering something for a friend, he kept saying, and he didn't know what he was carrying.

Yeah, yeah. The officers weren't buying it. Not from a rock star. . . . Tell us another.

So they grabbed his bag, opened it up, removed the contraband, ripped it open—and found six bags of gourmet dog food.

"☞ E ☜"

ON ELECTIONS, SNEAKY:

The race for city judge in Anderson, Indiana, deserves mention for either extreme stupidity—or amazing creativity—on the parts of those running.

City Judge Donald R. Phillippe was up for reelection and was running against two opponents in the Democratic primary. Polls indicated that Phillippe was way ahead, due to name recognition. So his two opponents filed petitions to change *their* names.

Opponent number one wanted to change his name to Donald R. Phillippe; opponent number two to . . . Donald R. Phillippe.

ON ELVIS IS ALIVE, PROOF OF:

There's always someone somewhere who claims to have had an Elvis sighting. Most people who claim to have seen Elvis still alive wind up calling the *National Enquirer*. Sometimes the people at the *Enquirer* follow up, but often they don't. However, this particular time they were definitely intrigued.

It wasn't the usual type of Elvis spotter, but a retired Harvard professor. And he said he had "irrefutable photographic evidence" that Elvis was actually alive.

So the *Enquirer* sent a reporter to the professor's remote home in the mountains of northern Vermont. When the reporter arrived, the elderly professor took him downstairs to the basement, where the professor unlocked the door to the room where he kept the evidence. Then finally the reporter was able to see it himself. It was one snapshot, a shot of the professor standing in front of the house—alone.

The reporter didn't get it. "Where's the photographic proof of Elvis?" he asked the professor.

"Well," replied the professor, "Elvis took the photo."

ON ENGLISH CHANNEL CROSSINGS:

In the late 1960s, Kenneth Blyton managed to successfully cross the English Channel in a metal bottle driven by a small motor. It was his third crossing, but his first time by bottle. When he landed at Cape Gris Nez, he laid out his next plan of attack.

"I have already crossed by bedstead and by barrel," he said. "Next year I intend to cross by giant banana."

On Environmental Scientists:

Scientists were puzzled. According to their state-of-the-art air pollution monitoring equipment worth hundreds of thousands of pounds, Newcastle, England, was by far the most polluted city in England—if not the world.

It was so polluted that the readings were literally off the charts. For two years, the scientists pondered: Why was this city's air so fantastically polluted? What could be causing this phenomenon?

It took a little time, but finally the answer became clear: The super air pollution monitoring machine had been placed right over a truck parking lot.

On Escapes, Not-So-Great:

Charles Haggard decided to rob one of those giant do-it-yourself home shopping centers.

But alert police caught him in the act and started to chase him. As Haggard ran, he saw a door. He opened it and ran through. Then he saw another door, which he opened and ran through, then another door. . . .

In all, Haggard ran through eleven fake doors before running into a brick wall and knocking himself out.

On Ethnic Liaison Officers, Not-So-Great:

In this age of cultural diversity, it's no wonder that new jobs have emerged that deal with multicultural issues.

For example, the principal ethnic liaison officer of the New South Wales, Australia, police force has the job of ensuring that everything runs smoothly between the police and the different ethnic groups of the area.

But the man who held this post in 1984 had a sort of unusual way of approaching his work:

"I see nothing wrong with calling people wogs, slopeheads, and gooks," he told the *Sydney Morning News*. "It's just a convenient way of identifying groups. . . . Nobody minds being called 'driver,' when the phrase 'Pull over, driver' is used. And as the only umbrella term for the groups is Southeast Asian Immigrant Community— which is a bit of a mouthful—I use wog, gook, etc.

"As a matter of fact, an Italian friend of mine told me that he feels quite comfortable being called a dago. He has been called a dago for thirty years and it saves him the trouble of explaining he is Italian. On the other hand, everybody knows what a dago means."

On Excuses by Eye Doctors, Bizarre:

An eye doctor was facing prosecution in a Belgian court. And as the good doctor's lawyer realized, the facts were the facts.

"What the prosecution says is technically true," the lawyer admitted to the court.

"Before prescribing contact lenses, my client, who is a state-registered optician, did indeed frequently order women to strip naked and dance around his consulting room while he played the accordion. However, there are mitigating circumstances to take into consideration. The fact is that the defendant qualified in England, where, he assures me, such techniques are commonplace."

The Belgian court acquitted the eye doctor.

On Excuses, Criminally Weak:

A criminal was arrested for burglary and breaking and entering. But he explained that it was all actually a mistake. "I felt tired," he said, "so I rested my head against the shop window and it fell in."

But what about police who saw him wearing a fur coat from the store? "I wore it to keep the dust off my sports coat."

And what about witnesses who saw him trying to knock a hole in the ceiling of the building? "I could not think of anything else to do at the time."

ON EXPLANATIONS, TOO PRECISE:

There's a time to be specific and a time to keep your mouth shut. Barry Shoemaker of Harlingen, Texas, learned it the hard way. He wound up being arrested because he was painstakingly specific.

To be more precise: Shoemaker was at a meeting of the Harlingen city commission, watching the proceedings and enjoying a smoke. The city manager noticed him in the audience and explained that no cigarette smoking was allowed. Would he please put it out?

Shoemaker got technical. "It's not a cigarette," he explained. "It's a joint."

ON EXPLORERS, BAD:

A man from Olive, Kentucky, had a dream. A dream that would take him away from the rolling hills of the Bluegrass State. The dream: to row across the icy Bering Strait, between Alaska and Russia, in a bathtub.

Unfortunately, the dream was not completely fulfilled. According to the explorer, "I took four gallons of peanut butter along, but on the morning of the fourth day it had gone solid. By late afternoon, although the sun was still high, the sea went rather thick. Next morning I was frozen in."

No problem. He abandoned the bathtub and walked to land.

ON EXPOSURE, STUPID:

"I am not scum," declared Jagdish Desai to the court in Singapore. "I admit I dropped my pants in front of this woman . . . but fate was to blame."

Jagdish's excuse for indecent exposure was a first in judicial history. It turns out he was walking near the subway station when he spied a mango tree. And then, as he put it: "I was hungry, so naturally I climbed [the tree] to pick some mangoes."

Naturally. But then Jagdish accidentally disturbed an ants' nest. And this is where his problems began.

As Jagdish explained: "When I got down, the ants began biting my private parts, so I went into the subway, took all my clothes off, and rubbed myself to brush them away. Any sane man would have done the same. Unfortunately, this woman happened by, completely misunderstood my intentions, and panicked. I invited her to come closer to see the ants for herself, but she only screamed and reported me to the station master, who had me arrested."

The judge evidently agreed. Desai's case was dismissed—"as long as accidental exposures don't occur again."

F

On Filmstrips, Brazilian-Style:

Back in November 1974, the famous movie *The Exorcist* came to La Pampa Cinema in Rio de Janeiro. But the audience soon was distracted by more than the devil possessing a little girl.

First, a rat began scampering about back and forth next to the screen stage, distracting viewers. The distraction got worse when an usherette, armed with a mop, began chasing the rat in front of the screen.

The angry crowd began yelling, "Take them off," meaning, of course, that the theater management should take the usherette, the mop, and the rat off the stage.

But the usherette didn't get the gist of the audience's words. She took them . . . more literally. After hitting the rat with the mop, she proceeded to take all her clothes off, and then, searching for something else to do, she started dancing nude in the projector light.

She stopped after the police arrived. As she explained to them, "I thought the audience was calling for me. I was as surprised as anyone."

On Flotation Devices, Dangers of:

It was another day at the seashore, when a dramatic sea rescue had to take place.

A little girl floated too far offshore on a pair of plastic inflatable teeth. She was rescued by a man—floating on an inflatable lobster.

Said a Coast Guard officer: "This sort of thing is all too common."

On Following Instructions, Literal Moments:

A young man named Will Smith was on line at Detroit's busy license bureau, patiently waiting for his turn to apply for a driver's license. Finally he reached the desk. The clerk shoved an application across to Smith and brusquely asked him to write his last name first and first name last.

Smith looked confused. "How's that again?"

"Like I said," the harried clerk said. "Write your name backward."

Good enough. Smith shrugged and followed orders, slowly writing "lliW htimS."

ON FOOTBALL GAMES AGAINST HEARING-IMPAIRED PLAYERS:

As a team of collegiate all-stars, the Norfolk Blues figured they knew it all when it came to football.

In 1912, they were up for a game against Galludet, the college for the hearing-impaired. The Blues figured it would be a piece of cake. Not only were they the all-stars, they were playing against people who couldn't hear.

So they flaunted their superiority for all it was worth. They didn't even bother huddling or calling signals. Their opponents were deaf, they reasoned, so why not openly talk about the plays they were running? No one would be able to hear them.

True, but they made one crucial error: The Galludet players could read lips.

The result? Norfolk was shut out—20 to 0.

G

ON GAS SIPHONING:

Siphoning gasoline out of a tank isn't exactly a job for the weak-stomached. Usually a person doing it sticks a siphoning tube into a tank and starts by sucking on the tube with his mouth. Often some gasoline is swallowed. It's not pleasant, but it's doable.

And this is what a thief intended to do in New Zealand in the spring of 1994.

An elderly couple at an East Coast campsite were awakened by sounds outside their mobile home. Too frightened to investigate what was going on, they stayed indoors, listening to the noises outside and waiting for morning. They went outside in the morning and realized that their fears had been well-founded. Outside of their mobile home, they found a siphoning hose, a gasoline can, and a metal cap from one of the tanks on the vehicle. Clearly, the thief had intended to siphon gasoline from the mobile home while its occupants were asleep. But the pool of vomit on the ground by the cap proved that something had gone wrong.

Putting the pieces together, they realized just what had happened:

The man had removed the cap from a tank, stuck the tube in, and started siphoning. But he had made a crucial error.

He had removed the cap from the sewage holding tank.

ON THE GERALDO SHOW, STUPID BREATHTAKING MOMENTS FROM:

Miami Vice was still one of the hottest shows on television. And Geraldo Rivera decided to do a news show revealing the *real* side of drug trafficking in the United States: "American Vice: The Doping of a Nation."

To make it even more dramatic and immediate, Rivera included a live segment showing a drug raid on a duplex. In this house, Rivera said on-air as viewers watched the cops ready to break in, "an alleged pimp and prostitute—a dude and his lady—real pros—are supplying truckers speed."

The cops burst into the house, followed closely by the camera crew, catching the entire dramatic incident live.

A woman, all alone, wearing a shirt and shorts, was painting the walls.

ON GETAWAYS:

It should have been a basic armed robbery. Two men from Edmonton, Canada, pulled into the Petro-Canada gas station in Vancouver, Canada, pulled their guns, locked the terrified attendant in the bathroom, and made off with $100. It was a clean getaway.

But twenty minutes later, the not-so-dynamic duo realized they were lost. Finally they decided to risk it and ask for directions, so they pulled into a gas station.

Somehow they didn't realize that they were at the same station they had robbed earlier—and the cashier they asked directions from was the man they had locked in the bathroom before. He played it cool, gave them directions, and, as soon as they started walking away again, he began calling the police.

Then the robbers returned yet another time.

This time their car wouldn't start—and they needed a mechanic. When they learned that there was no mechanic on until eight the following morning, they kept trying to start the car themselves.

The police finally arrived and the crooks were still there. This time they were on the phone, trying to call a tow truck.

Their battery had finally given out.

ON GETAWAYS, FAILED:

After robbing a tavern in New Athens, Illinois, at gunpoint, the robber ran outside to his getaway car. But in the excitement of the robbery, he had lost his keys. What to do?

Better thieves might run—but this man had an even better idea. He stripped off his clothes to his underwear and went back inside the tavern, saying that he had been robbed, too.

Unfortunately, despite a dismal attempt at disguising his voice, absolutely everyone in the tavern recognized him. He was arrested.

ON GETTING THE VOTE OUT, OVERZEALOUS ATTEMPTS AT:

Herbert Connolly wanted to keep his seat on the Massachusetts Governor's Council badly . . . *very* badly.

So he did what many candidates do: He campaigned vigorously right to the last minute. He raced around, making speeches, shaking hands, and urging people to rush to the polls and vote.

He was so busy doing all this that, by the time he got to the voting booth himself, it had been closed for fifteen minutes.

The good news was that all that extra campaigning netted him 14,715 votes. The bad news was that his opponent got 14,716.

On Getting Too Close to the Story, the Media:

On June 9, 1978, Mr. Bob Specas was ready to beat a domino record by knocking down 100,000 dominoes in a row.

The media was there to broadcast the historic event. A TV camera recorded his progress as Specas set up the last dominoes for his performance.

97,497 . . . 97,498 . . . 97,499. Then a TV cameraman dropped his press badge . . . and the dominoes went off.

On Golf Holes, Hard-to-Sink:

Some people just never give up.

One case in point: It was the qualifying round of the Shawnee Invitational for Ladies at Shawnee-on-Delaware, Pennsylvania. One contestant was on her sixteenth hole, which was a par four—that is, it took pros four strokes on average to make the hole.

The contestant teed off and the ball soared . . . straight into the nearby river.

A normal golfer would take the penalty and try again. But this dauntless contestant felt differently. When she saw the ball floating down the river, she got into a rowboat and ordered her husband to start rowing.

Standing in the boat, she began hacking at the floating ball with her golf club. Her husband kept on rowing and she kept on hacking—and counting.

Everyone else had forgotten about her, when she finally managed to get the ball onto dry land. Accompanied by a shout of "Fore," her ball came whizzing toward the green from a totally unexpected direction.

She managed to sink the ball into the hole without a further hitch . . . two hours and 166 strokes after starting.

On Golf, Need for a Hard Head When Playing:

It was the final round of the 1934 U.S. Open and the pressure was on. Bobby Cruickshank was two strokes ahead of his competitors. He had to make the next hole in four strokes to keep his lead.

Cruickshank's drive off the tee was fine. But his following approach shot was too weak. With horror, he watched the ball sink with a splash into the stream in front of the green—and his heart sank along with it.

A split second later, the ball bounced back out of the water— apparently ricocheting off of a submerged rock—and rolled onto the green only ten feet from the hole.

It was a miracle. With a whoop, Cruickshank tossed his club

in the air, tipped his hat, and yelled to the heavens, "Thank you, God!"

That's when Cruickshank got his second shock of the day.

The club, so cheerfully tossed into the air, began hurtling earthward. It came down hard, cracked him on the head, and knocked him to the ground.

He managed to get up again, but he couldn't regain his steadiness. After his great start, he wound up finishing third.

ON GREENGROCERY DISPLAYS, NONE-TOO-APPETIZING:

A woman from Stackstead, England, had owned a greengrocery for years. It was her life—so much so that her fondest wish was to be laid out in state on the counter when she died.

And her instructions were followed to the letter.

"It was a very beautiful occasion," said one friend. "Margaret lay in state on the counter for two days. Many regular customers came in to pay their respects, and the lying-in ended up with a service in the shop conducted underneath her favorite poster that depicted a large Jersey potato."

SPECIAL SECTION

● ●

GOVERNMENT GAFFES

I don't make jokes. I just watch the government and report the facts.

—WILL ROGERS

No one said it better than Will Rogers back in the 1930s. Humorists searching for material have little more to do than go to Washington or to their nearest town hall meeting to see stupidity in action.

Of course, we the people foot the bill for all this. And that's why, in order for you to get your money's worth out of your tax dollars, we've included this section.

The government may no longer keep the streets safe, the garbage collected, or your family healthy. But they can still dish out the laughs.

☞ Governor William Donald Schaefer of Maryland decided to raise the morale of his state, so he appointed a task force on self-esteem. After eighteen months of study, the task force reported that it had identified exactly 1,050 things that Maryland residents were doing to make each other feel better about themselves. Unfortunately, the task force also concluded that it didn't have the money to let any Maryland residents know just what these 1,050 things were.

☞ The Indiana State Police instituted an intensive three-month investigation into the suspicious death of one man. Their findings after their in-depth investigation: The man, who had died of thirty-two hammer blows to the head, was *not* a suicide but the victim of a murder.

☞ A post office in Ohio discovered that they hadn't done their bit to spread holiday good cheer. About twelve thousand letters were stamped with YOU BITCH instead of MERRY CHRISTMAS before the error was discovered.

☞ The Pennsylvania state government introduced a bill in late 1994 to take care of a pressing matter—that of people "libeling" fruits, vegetables, and seafood. Under the proposed bill, growers, manufacturers, and marketers of perishable food could "attempt to recover damages for the disparagement of any such food product or commodity."

☞ The Wildlife Division of Ohio spent over $25,000 in wages tracking down a notorious criminal. A team of fourteen agents and two undercover agents spent three weeks on the job—keeping surveillance, taking photographs from nearby bushes, even buying products undercover from the criminal . . . who happened to be an eight-year-old boy who had committed the heinous act of selling illegal bait. The boy had a stand outside his parents' house from which he sold worms to passing fishermen. It turned out that, aside from the two undercover agents, he had sold bait to only four fishermen. The case was dismissed—but it had cost Ohio enough money to buy twenty-seven tons of worms.

☞ In 1978, State Representative John Galbraith of Ohio came up with a novel idea for reducing energy usage: He introduced a bill to abolish January and February. His reasoning: "If we divided the fifty-nine extra days between July and August, we will cut our energy needs by about one-third through eliminating the coldest days of the year. Cold is largely a psychological matter. If people look at the calendar and see that it is July, they will be quite happy to turn the heat down."

☞ In 1990, the Houston city council wanted to draft an ordinance to outlaw bare women's breasts. To make sure the language was just so, they hired a researcher. His task—to detail why women's breasts are different than men's.

☞ In the late 1980s, New York State-owned Long Island Lighting Company notified the Nuclear Regulatory Commission about their evacuation plan for residents in the event of an accident at the Shoreham nuclear power plant. The plan? Area residents would be immediately evacuated to the Nassau Coliseum—unless, of course, the coliseum was being used for a hockey game, ice show, or circus performance.

☞ The city council of Longmont, Colorado, apparently is hesitant to offend anyone in its jurisdiction. As proof of their unwillingness to cast a pall on anyone's day, they voted to replace all signs referring to "dead-end streets," fearing that people might find them macabre. In their place, they would put up signs reading: NO OUTLET.

☞ How many famous Thai badminton players can you name? When you say "badminton," do you automatically think of Thailand? Evidently, questions like this bothered Thailand's Minister of Health back in 1979. He was quite worried about the low level of badminton playing in his country. The problem, the minister finally deduced, was due to the lack of shuttlecocks. In his words: "Time and time again, I have said that unless shuttlecocks are freely available to the people of Thailand, it will be almost impossible to increase the national badminton standard. At the present time, there are less than five hundred shuttlecocks in the country.

This is the reason why the number of Thai badminton players has not matched our kingdom's population explosion."

Readers will be glad to know that today Thailand has thousands of shuttlecocks, no doubt due to the Minister of Health, who cared enough to make badminton a priority.

☞ Three small figurines in an exhibit at Dallas City Hall happened to be nude. So the thoughtful city officials, worried that the nudity might offend some viewers, had the figurines covered with tiny handmade fig leaves.

☞ After Florida passed an "English-only" law, counties weren't allowed to spend public funds on offering services in any foreign languages. Eager to comply to the letter, Dade County went a bit overboard: The Dade County zoo stopped including Latin names of animal species on any of its signs.

☞ The Pentagon spent $3,000 on a six-month study to answer this burning question: Do umbrellas detract from the appearance of military officers?

☞ The Wisconsin state government asked a different burning question in 1976. The state's Law Enforcement Assistance Association spent over $200,000 asking criminals to answer why they wished to escape punishment.

☞ Excessive noise from jets landing and taking off from Toledo Airport, located near Toledo, Ohio, was causing problems for residents. So, in November 1994, Toledo Mayor Carty Finkeimer came up with a simple solution: The city should try to relocate deaf people in the high-noise area. To make this plan feasible, he suggested that the city actually help facilitate the purchase of the houses from the complainers. The idea didn't fly with the public . . . and a few days later the mayor apologized for his suggestion.

☞ In a somewhat related vein, NASA officials were apparently surprised when they couldn't find any volunteers for their latest experiment—studying the effects of blasting jet airplane noise into private homes for fourteen hours a day.

☞ It was a tough decision: What time of day should the Waco, Texas, city council begin their meetings? After a great deal of back and forth debate, one council member came up with a clever idea that might solve their problem. Maybe the *public* should decide the issue. So the council voted on whether there should be a public referendum on the time of day issue—and the vote was a 3 to 3 tie.

☞ Ten thousand birds were infesting a garbage dump in Cynon Valley, England—and the town council was going crazy. All attempts at scaring away the birds had failed. The council finally decided to contact the Ministry of Agriculture and ask for assistance. And after six months of intensive field study, the scientists employed by the ministry came up with the following helpful suggestions: (1) A dummy of a man should be hauled to the top of a mast and exploded—four times a day; (2) Bulldozers used on the garbage dump should be equipped with radios "permanently tuned to classical music"; (3) Council workmen should stand around the dump during the day and throw stones at the birds. A fourth recommendation that was finally cut from the scientists' list proposed that "tasty scraps soaked in hashish oil be scattered over the dump." But the idea was scrapped because "after a recent trial of this method, several birds fell out of the sky like bricks."

☞ This excerpt from an education article in *The San Francisco Chronicle* should shed light on the doings of boards of education:

"The California Board of Education will meet in secret next week to decide if it may meet in secret. No one is saying what the meeting is about. That, according to a school-board spokesman, is a secret. Secret meetings by public agencies are common. Secret meetings about secret meetings, although legal, are less common. Public announcements about secret meetings are required by law.

It's all explained in Government Code Section 11126(q)2(a) . . . 'The California State Board of Education reserves the right to meet in closed session pursuant to Government Code Section 11126(q)2(a) to determine whether the facts and circumstances authorize it to meet in closed session pursuant to Government Code Section 11126(q)2(a).' "*

☞ In May 1994, the Islamic sect Tebrik-a-Nifaz in Pakistan announced that true Muslims should drive on the right side of the road—and sect followers did just that. The problem? Everyone else in Pakistan drives on the left side of the road. Two weeks later, the sect put out another announcement rescinding the previous one since there were so many accidents.

☞ Instead of Stonehenge, why not Foamhenge? This compelling thought comes courtesy of an English local government leader, who conceived it as an employment project for out-of-work laborers. Workers would recreate the English stone monument in polystyrene foam, and "the real monument could be left in its quiet glory."

* Excerpted in the *Progressive*, March 1995.

H

On Hamlet, Stupid Innovations in:

Keswick Polytechnic in England probably put on the stupidest version ever of Shakespeare's *Hamlet* back in 1975.

First of all, the length was cut to fifteen minutes.

Second, it was renamed *Hamlette,* because the producers couldn't find enough male actors.

Third, they gave Claudia, Hamlette's aunt, most of Polonius' lines, because the actress playing Claudia learned his lines by mistake.

Fourth, they added some bizarre new parts to the play: Hamlette's sister Joyce, along with her friend Dinah, whose lines are taken from *Romeo and Juliet,* "with the dirt removed." Finally they added a unique new character, Louise—a girl disguised as a male deaf-mute person who drowns herself.

On Hand Grenades, Hard-to-Handle:

Every so often a brilliant designer comes up with a revolutionary new weapon that changes history forever. Less often a not-too-smart designer comes up with a really stupid weapon. A weapon like Hand Grenade Number 74 (ST).

This grenade was designed by experts during World War II to blow up tanks better than regular grenades. Regular grenades are made of hard metal, and they usually bounce against enemy tanks when thrown.

The Number 74 (ST) was different, its proud designers explained. It had a special coating so it would *stick* to the enemy tanks. All the top brass and experts loved it. It was revolutionary.

In all the excitement, no one really bothered thinking about a minor question: What happened to the sticky grenade *before* it got stuck to an enemy tank?

The quick answer: It got stuck to the soldier *throwing* it. Troops using the grenade during battle found that out quickly. They usually had about five seconds to unstick themselves before the grenade that was stuck to their hands or clothes exploded.

Needless to say, there weren't many reorders for new supplies of Hand Grenade Number 74 (ST).

ON HICCUP CURES, DEFINITIVE:

Squire John Mytton, a nineteenth-century English sportsman, was known for his love of drinking. His good friend, Nimrod the biographer, called him "Mango, the King of the Pickles." Mytton had taken to the bottle at age ten and was known to put away about eight quarts of port a day.

But his drinking brought about the usual drawbacks—he was a reckless driver, he was prone to accidents, and he frequently got the hiccups.

One night he was in his bedroom when a particularly irritating fit of hiccups struck him. How best to rid himself of these pesky hiccups? Mytton drunkenly thought about it as he undressed, then came up with a novel solution: He would frighten them away by setting fire to his shirt. He picked up a candle, put it next to his shirt, and watched the shirt go up in flames.

The cure worked, but there was one drawback. Mytton was inside the shirt at the time.

Two servants heard his yelling, ran to his room, ripped the shirt off, and smothered the flames. The drunken Mytton went to bed— burned but pleased by his success. As he put it: "The hiccup is gone, by God."

ON HIJACKING ATTEMPTS:

In 1976, a hijacker got up from his airline seat. He took out a gun and held up a stewardess.

"Take me to Detroit," he said.

"But we're going to Detroit already," said the stewardess.

"Oh, good," said the hijacker and sat back down.

ON HOBBIES, ODD PROJECTILE-INVOLVING:

In 1988, two young men in the north of England invented a machine that threw gasoline-soaked toilets at country fairs. They were immortalized in a local newspaper article headlined: THOSE MAGNIFICENT MEN AND THEIR FLAMING LATRINES.

And it gave their cousin and weapons enthusiast Hew Kennedy of Shropshire, England, an idea: If his cousins could make a hit slinging flaming toilets into the air, why not try building something bigger that would sling even larger projectiles?

So, with the investment of $17,000 and the help of his neighbor Richard Barr, Kennedy came up with a full-scale reconstruction of a trebuchet—a sixty-foot-tall medieval siege engine. He started flinging anything large he could get his hands on—pigs, pianos, horses. Dead pigs went a good 175 yards. The longest piano fling was 151 yards. Dead horses only went about 100 yards at best.

He tried to get the producers of Kevin Costner's *Robin Hood: Prince of Thieves* interested in using his machine, but to no avail. And he also toyed with the thought of selling the idea to the operator of an

American theme park—to sling cars. (His reasoning: "It's an amusement in America to smash up motor cars, isn't it?")

His final great idea—slinging live humans. Kennedy knew that in medieval days they sent ambassadors over castle walls via catapult. So why not devise this as a thrill ride for modern people? Early experiments with pigs weren't promising, though. One pig carcass exploded. Finally a few hogs were successfully launched and retrieved. No word on whether he actually tried it with a human.

Finally, by the end of 1991, the thrill was gone. "I'm bloody bored with it now," he said to one interviewer. The problem? He had already flung pretty much anything that could be flung.

But he hadn't completely given up his hobby. His newest idea—building a giant crossbow that would use telegraph poles for arrows.

ON HOLDUPS, NECESSITY OF KEEPING GUN IN:

Wazie Jiwi, a Houston convenience store clerk, was being held up by a robber holding two pistols.

Thinking quickly, he offered the robber $100 for the guns. The robber agreed. Jiwi pulled the money from the cash register, handed the money over, and took the guns the robber gave him.

Then he turned one of the guns on the robber and demanded the money back.

On Holdups, Necessity of Obtaining Gun in:

It seemed like the typical armed robbery. A man rushed into a grocery store, glared at the owner behind the counter, and yelled the typical: "Give me your money or I'll shoot!"

The owner, Mohammed Razzaq, almost complied. But something bothered him. Then he had it.

"Where's your gun?" he asked.

The would-be robber tried to brass it out on technicalities. He didn't actually *have* a gun with him, he admitted, but he would go *get* a gun if Razzaq gave him any more problems.

With that not-so-threatening promise, the man slunk out.

On Holiday Promotions, Unseasonal:

The Great Challenge Superstore in Grange Hall Bay, California, had a boffo promotional idea to draw the crowds in during Easter: an Easter Santa.

But it didn't quite work out the way the promotions officer planned.

"I admit our attempt to introduce an Easter Santa has gone wrong," she later said.

It started smoothly. The Easter Santa pulled up outside the store as planned, ensconced in his Egg Sleigh.

But then one passerby apparently didn't take to the sight. He went after the Easter Santa with a golf club. All the children who had lined up waiting for Santa began to boo, to cry, or to run away.

"But we are not giving in," the plucky promotions officer promised, "and will be thinking of new ways to promote the Santa concept."

ON HOLLYWOOD MOGULS:

A producer was pitching an idea to movie mogul Sam Goldwyn—a film adaptation of the book *The Making of Yesterday: The Diaries of Raoul de Roussy de Sales, 1938–1942.* As he kept selling the idea, pointing out why the diary would make a great film, he noticed that Goldwyn wouldn't stop staring at the book.

"How do you like that?" Goldwyn finally mused out loud. "Four years old and the kid keeps a diary."

On Honeymoons, Surprising:

Marcel Valjean and his new wife were spending a wonderful honeymoon on the lovely tropical island of Réunion in June 1977.

On the night of June 7, Valjean was returning from a midnight stroll while his wife was softly slumbering in their beautiful honeymoon cottage. As he came to the fence surrounding their tropical love nest, Valjean had an amusing idea. Why not vault over the fence into the cottage and surprise his slumbering bride?

Unfortunately, the night was dark and what Valjean thought was the fence near his honeymoon cottage was not the fence in question. Valjean instead vaulted over a fence surrounding the deadly crater of a nearby volcano—and died.

On Hot Dog Storage Spots:

Sports fans are an excitable lot. So much so that, sometimes, they're so intent on the game that they just don't seem to know what they're doing.

That must have been the case with one British soccer fan, an enthusiastic supporter of the Chelsea team.

He was fined £10 for sticking a hot dog up the anus of a police horse named Eileen.

But there was a good *reason* for it all. "I was overcome with excitement after the match. I wanted to get rid of the hot dog, and just at that moment, Eileen wandered by. I intended no harm and am a genuine animal lover."

On Hymns, Interesting Translations of:

Missionaries in Nigeria in the 1800s ran into a few problems translating Christian hymns into the languages of Nigeria. They hadn't grasped the basic fact that in some languages of Nigeria, different tones or pitches give words completely different meanings. And so for many years the missionaries had the Igbo people of Nigeria singing favorite hymns like: "God's pig, which is never shared," and the not-so-stirring hymn that begins: "There is no egg on the bicycle."

ON IDEAL BIBLE FAMILIES, DUBIOUS:

One year the Cheshire Baptist Association decided to set up a side-show at the Lancashire Agricultural Fair—a tableau of mannequins showing the "Ideal Bible Family" at home.

The problem? Where would the association get the figures they needed?

Not to worry. Help came in the form of a Madame Tussaud's Wax Museum in nearby Blackpool. The manager arranged for the fully dressed mannequins to be delivered to the fair, where the association quickly set them up and opened their doors to the public.

The whole setup seemed perfect for the "Let's get back to family values" theme. Viewers saw the stern but gentle father, the innocent young daughter, and the sweet loving mother sitting around a table in a humble room, looking down at the opened family Bible. And by their side, pointing at the chosen biblical passage, was the wise Baptist minister.

But most of the viewers had the nagging feeling they had seen the members of this "Ideal Bible Family" before. . . .

They were right. The association was shocked to discover that the mannequins were not your basic average God-fearing Baptists.

Instead, the wax dummy of the innocent daughter had the head and face of Snow White. The mother had the body of Queen Elizabeth and the head of a famous ice skater. The father was a well-known swindler. And as for the minister—he was the notorious murderer Dr. Crippen.

ON INSECTICIDE, SWALLOWING:

A Turkish farmer was taken to the hospital with severe stomach pains.

After examining him, the doctor was very confused. Apparently, the farmer was suffering because he had swallowed insecticide. But there was only a very small amount in his system, which ruled out a suicide attempt. So how—or why—had the man ingested insecticide?

The farmer explained that it had been no accident. He had deliberately taken insecticide. And for good reason.

He had accidentally swallowed a fly. "I wanted to kill it before it reproduced inside of me," he said.

ON THE IRS:

The IRS demanded $159.78 in penalties from George Witteier for underpaying his tax. He was off by a penny.

ON THE IRS, A MUCH, MUCH FRIENDLIER VERSION OF:

As a public service to taxpayers, the Internal Revenue Service provides a free tax information service by phone. All you have to do is call the 800 number listed in your local directory, and you can get your tax questions answered.

But callers in Portland, Oregon, got a different type of service. Instead of the usual bureaucratic greeting, Portland taxpayers heard a sultry voice breathing, "Hi, sexy."

The embarrassed IRS later explained that there had been a little mix-up. The Portland phone directory had misprinted the number. Instead of the IRS, callers were reaching Phone Phantasies.

SPECIAL SECTION

Idiotic Inventions and Products We Could Live Without

"Necessity is the mother of invention." This old saying reveals the basic idea about inventing: As an inventor, you see a need or a problem, and then you try to invent something to fulfill that need or solve that problem. Invention's modern-day cousin, new product development, is no different.

But there are always a few inventors or product developers out there who march to a completely different drummer. They aren't going to ask themselves questions like: Is it useful? Would anyone need it? Do people really *want* a combined cockroach trap and cheese grater?

No, these people boldly go forward, blithely ignoring convention, practicality, market research, and basic common sense.

And so we have these brilliantly obtuse innovators to thank for this collection of utterly ridiculous inventions and products.

☞ **the Further Life Memory Service:** A unique service thought up by Darren West of Fairport, New York. His company sends out birthday cards to people you designate, and they receive the cards each year . . . after you've died. As he put it, "Just think, though you passed away months ago, your family will get a card saying: 'On this special day of your life, take joy in the fact that those who have traveled on before would give anything to be in your shoes.'" The cost? A reasonable $25 a year. Prepaid, of course.

☞ **the Tonya Tapper:** Named in honor of ice skating's notorious Tonya Harding. Minneapolis lawyer David Anderson came up with the idea after hearing about the steel club Harding's henchman whacked Nancy Kerrigan with—and began marketing his own steel club by mail, for only $39.95 (plus shipping and handling). As he said in the *Minneapolis–St. Paul Star Tribune,* the Tonya Tapper might be "the seed crystal for similar personal security products—a whole line of batons, with different colors, holsters, and grips—even one of key chain size."

☞ *Packed and Stacked:* A 1994 calendar put out by Watergate conspirator and talk-show host G. Gordon Liddy, featuring young voluptuous women in scanty bathing suits or lingerie. The twist? They're holding high-powered weapons. (Note: Liddy promised that $30,000 from the sales of the calendar would go to a fund for victims of the 1995 Oklahoma City bombing.)

☞ **a Musical Bra for Mozart Buffs:** Manufactured by Japanese lingerie maker Triumph International, this bra was created to honor Mozart on the two hundredth anniversary of his death. The bra contains a memory chip that plays a twenty-second selection of Mozart's music and also has lights that flash in time as the music plays. One drawback: The bra isn't washable, so it's not for everyday wear.

☞ **Insecticide Pantyhose:** Bug-resistant pantyhose that repels spiders, cockroaches, and other crawling pests. Introduced in the late 1980s by Kanebo, a Japanese textile and cosmetics company, this product actually caught on, selling over four hundred thousand pairs in the first few months. It costs only about $2 a pair.

☞ **Sweet Jesus Chocolate:** Chocolate crucifixes with a Christ figure that bleeds red jelly when bitten into. Answering critics who claim this candy was in poor taste, its producer, a Canberra, Australia, confectioner, explained that "The object . . . is to put religion back into Easter with an edible icon. People who are offended by the icon have lost touch with reality. A Sweet Jesus crucifix will remind them that Easter is more than three days on the beach."

☞ **Artificial Spray-On Dirt:** An enterprising West Germany firm came up with this clever product for all those urbanites who drive four-wheel-drive and other Jeep-type vehicles and want them to look rugged, as if they were actually used on something other than congested city streets.

☞ **Grenade Shampoo:** A manly man's shampoo, packaged in a bottle that looks just like a grenade. As the ad copy stated: "Pull the pin. You'll know it's real!"

☞ **Freeze-Dried Pets:** Offered by Preserv-A-Pet. Firm owner Roger Saatzer put it succinctly: "The next best thing to bringing [your pet] back to life is to have it freeze-dried." With this thought in mind, his company freeze-dries dead household pets for their heartbroken owners to keep. Costs range from $450 for a basic sitting cat up to $2,000 for an attacking German shepherd.

☞ **the .45 Semiautomatic Telephone:** Even the company that produced this telephone that looked like a gun admitted it might be a tough sell. Said Jammie Tizzard, an official of Covina, California-based S. W. Productions: "It will be a little shocking to walk into a room and see someone holding a gun to his head, talking into it. But like anything else, the public will get used to it." Apparently not. How many of these phones do you see today?

☞ **a One-of-a-Kind Replica of a World War I Trench:** For sale in the late 1980s by the Herbert Hoover Presidential Library and Museum in West Branch, Iowa. For only $7,500, you get a real-life thirty-by-eight-foot replica of a World War I trench, "complete with high-tech sound and lighting effects, robotic soldier, and periscopes with stereoscopic battlefield scenes." An added plus: It's wheelchair-accessible.

☞ **Drive-Through Visiting Booths at Funeral Homes:** Offered by Gatling's Funeral Home in Chicago, among others. This nifty innovation allows mourners to sign the register and view the body live (well, sort of) on a video screen—all without leaving the comfort of their cars. It's great for people who have difficulty walking, those who want to pay their respects quickly, and those who want to remain incognito for some reason. As the owner of Gatling's put it: "This way the girlfriend can go through the drive-through and pay her respects in whatever name she chooses, while the wife is inside with the deceased. It happens all the time."

☞ **Coffin with Escape Hatch:** The perfect product for those cautious souls who fear getting buried alive. Newark, New Jersey, inventor Franz Vester invented this in 1868. It's a coffin with a lid and a tube that "extends from the coffin up through and over the surface of the grave, said tube containing a ladder and cord, one end of said cord being placed in the hand of the person laid in the coffin, and the other end of said cord being attached to a bell on top of the square tube, so that, should a person be interred ere life is extinct, he can, on recovery to consciousness, ascend from the grave and the coffin by the ladder; or, if not able to ascend by said ladder, ring the bell, thereby giving an alarm, and thus save himself from premature burial and death."

☞ **Bird Diaper:** Just what it sounds like. It was designed in 1959 by Milwaukee inventor Bertha Dlugi in response to what she obviously thought was a problem: Pet birds were often allowed to fly through an owner's house, yet "These birds cannot normally be house-trained as other pets are, and their excremental discharge is frequently deposited on household furnishings when they are at liberty, creating an unsanitary condition." The answer to this? The bird diaper, a triangular patch of material attached to a harness that you can put around your pet parakeet or whatever.

☞ **Wind Bag:** A genteel name for a not-so-genteel product. The wind bag, invented in 1939, was designed "for the receiving and storing gas formed by the digestion of foods." In other words, it is a fart collector. It consists of a tube with a nipple on it that you put in "one end of the alimentary tract" (or your rectum, as the drawing with the patent application showed) and a collection chamber at the other end of the tube. It included a muffler (for obvious reasons) and a handy strap or belt that enabled you to discreetly wear the device under your clothes. Apparently (and we can't imagine why), this product never caught on.

☞ **Rat Bell:** Another attempt by humankind to build a better mouse-trap. This invention, designed in 1908, never caught on—and probably for good reason. The inventors, Joseph Barad and Edward Markoff, envisioned a fairly humane way of getting rid of mice or rats, but you have to wonder about its efficacy. The invention was a spring-resisted tripping device. When a mouse or rat set off the trap, its head would go through a frame, where a band with a bell on it would encircle its neck. The animal is then freed—but is now wearing a collar with a bell. As the inventors explained in their application: " 'The bell-rat,' as it may be termed, then in seeking its burrow or colony announces his coming by the sounds emitted by the bell, thereby frightening the other rats and causing them to flee, thus practically exterminating them in a sure and economical manner."

☞ **Tingle Pants:** A stupid name for a truly stupid product. Designed for music lovers (apparently) who liked getting a real thrill as they listened to their sound systems. Tingle Pants (also called "Rock 'n' Roll Pants") were black Lycra bikini underwear—for both men and women—with a stereo speaker in the crotch! You would wear the bikini and plug it into the output mode of your stereo and feel the vibrations in your crotch. They cost only $20, but they never really caught on, maybe because they were a little unwieldy—or maybe because no one wanted to feel the beat in their crotch.

☞ **the Two-Potato Clock:** A clock run by potatoes . . . or oranges . . . or even beer. More specifically, this 1984 product was a digital clock that ran off the energy generated by two electrodes implanted in any acidic medium (like a potato). Time ran out quickly for this one.

☞ **Pussyfoot:** A cat feeder probably best-suited for people who secretly hate their cats. This product was introduced in 1979 and was an acrylic cat food dispenser that made feeding the cat a simple chore. You put food into the feeder and it would automatically dispense to the cat. Great idea for a pet owner—but not so great for the cat. The lid of the feeder had a nasty tendency to flip down while the cat was eating and hit it on the nose.

☞ **Snif-T-Panties:** Women's underwear impregnated with fragrance . . . and not just the obvious floral fragrances, either. Snif-T-Panties (developed in 1975 by a Miami company) were offered in a range of scents, including the predictable rose, as well as banana, popcorn, pickles, pizza, and . . . to please the drinkers, whiskey!

☞ **the Floater Bubble:** A device enabling fishermen to go far from the riverbank and stay safe, or even to cross a stream without getting wet. This watertight suit was introduced in 1954 by Minnoqua, an American company, and included an adjustable strap seat and large rubber ring. It did keep anglers dry, but not without risk on the part of the wearer: The fisherman wearing his Floater Bubble could easily get caught in strong winds or currents and get carried far away from the fish he was pursuing.

☞ **Dog Glasses:** Ever worry about Fido's eyesight? This invention, patented by a French optician in 1975, is the answer. The inventor developed them after she made sunglasses for her own dog. Just like glasses for people, they can be adjusted to different visual deficiencies—there are corrective lenses for myopic dogs; glasses for dogs recuperating from cataracts; even protective ones against wind and dust for dogs who hang their heads out of car windows.

☞ and **Horse Glasses:** A great bet for racehorses who just can't see straight. The patent for these was registered in 1979 and covers both corrective lenses or plain old tinted lenses, both of which also protect against dust, mud, sand, and so on. The inventor claims that the optical assistance from these glasses results in better performance from the horse, because it's calmer and steadier now that it can see.

☞ **the Motorized Bar Stool:** A 1976 invention that's perfect for people who enjoy bellying up to the bar but who hate changing positions. With your motorized bar stool, you can zip around without ever getting up from your stool. An added plus: It has rear disc brakes.

☞ **the Combined Plow-Gun:** A handy product that lets farmers have "at hand an efficient weapon of defense" while plowing the fields. An added bonus: It's also "symmetrical and pleasing to the eye."

☞ **the Ultimate "It Dices, It Shreds, It Grates" as Seen on TV:** This invention, bearing patent no. 586025, is a combined grater, shredder, slicer—and mouse and fly trap.

☞ **a Fishing Lure with a Little Mirror in It:** This patent, no. 23,351, was registered in 1916. The application states: "A male fish seeing his image . . . will appear to see another fish approach it from the opposite end with the intent to seize the bait, and this will not only arouse his warlike spirit, but also appeal to his greed, and he will seize the bait quickly." As an added little touch, the inventor made the mirror slightly convex so that the mirror image is smaller—just "in case the fish is suspected of cowardice."

☞ **the Eight-Function Bicycle:** Designed by a Chinese inventor from the Dongling Machinery Plant in Shenyang. By twisting various levers, this versatile vehicle can become a tricycle, a bicycle that pedals backward, a wheelchair, a sofa, a desk, an easel, and a tripod for cameras.

☞ J ☜

On Journalism Students, Ones Not Bound for The New York Times:

In 1995, undergraduate journalism students at Arizona State University were given a quiz, including names that every aspiring journalist should recognize. Here are some of the answers:

- Alzheimer's: Imported beer.
- Apartheid: A building in Athens.
- Louis Armstrong: The first man on the moon.
- Count Basie: A vampire.
- Jesse Jackson: The leader of the Moral Majority.

On Juror Instructions, Suggestive:

It was a rape case in the 1970s and the victim was on the stand. As she testified, the judge noticed that one male juror was dozing. He paused and asked the victim to repeat what her attacker had said.

The victim shook her head. She was too embarrassed to repeat it. "Okay," the judge said, "write down what the attacker said on a piece of paper."

The victim did so, and this piece of paper was passed to the jury. One by one, each member took the paper, unfolded it, and read the rapist's statement, which went something like: "Tonight I'm going to blank you like you've never been blanked before."

Sitting next to the sleepy juror, who had gone back to dozing, was a beautiful female juror. It was her turn to read what the rapist had said. She got the paper, unfolded it, read it, then folded it again. She nudged the sleeping juror awake and handed him the paper.

He sleepily unfolded it and read the message. The expression on his face changed into something close to absolute joy. He turned and looked at the beautiful blonde woman. He winked at her as he stuffed the piece of paper in his pocket.

When the judge asked him for it, he blushed and shook his head. It was a personal matter, he explained.

ON JURY DUTY, WHY PEOPLE VOLUNTEER FOR:

It was a difficult case back in the early 1970s—whether to pronounce the owners of the Bottoms Up Club of New York City guilty of obscenity.

So New York Judge Irving Nathan decided to take the jury to the club and see the allegedly obscene act.

The judge and jury watched the act once—focusing on the part where a sexy couple performed the "Dance of Love," with a climactic scene of lovemaking on a bearskin rug. The jury was unable to decide definitely whether it was obscene. So the jury members asked to see the act one more time. They watched it carefully again. But they still couldn't reach a decision. So this time they asked the understudies to perform the same act one more time.

Fortunately, the police involved in the case were very understanding. According to Detective Gil Powers: "It *is* a difficult matter. The police have watched the show seventy-five times."

K

ON KNOCKOUTS, PSYCHIC:

In 1977, a daredevil with a twist appeared on the scene: a woman who billed herself as the Psychic Escapologist. She not only performed death-defying stunts, she used her incredible powers of ESP to direct her through them.

In March 1977 she was going to do one of her most amazing stunts of all: the sixty-mile-per-hour blindfold dash. She would drive 60 mph over a measured mile while wearing an iron blindfold.

It started without a hitch. She put on the blindfold, started driving, and, in her own words, "no sooner had I started than I felt myself reading the mind of someone in the crowd. This thought-transferee began by giving me explicit instructions. But just as the alarm bell told me I had reached fifty, they stopped beaming."

With no psychic instructions, the Psychic Escapologist crashed into the corner of a barn and was knocked unconscious.

She suffered extensive injuries, and while recovering in the hospital the disillusioned daredevil announced that she would no longer be repeating that particular stunt because "you can no longer rely on people."

But all was not lost. As she assured fans, she would still do the other part of her act, in which she escaped from a large polyethylene bag in twenty minutes.

ON KNOCKOUTS, UNUSUAL:

C. D. Blaylock was a heavyweight boxer at Louisiana State University in the early 1930s. Six feet tall, the boxer was noted for his unusually long reach.

One night in the ring he was facing a shorter and stockier opponent from Missouri State. In the second round, Blaylock came at his opponent with a strong right. Since it looked as if it would be a knockout if it landed, his opponent quickly tried to avoid the punch by moving in closer to Blaylock. But as he did this, his head hit Blaylock's right elbow.

This acted like a lever, adding even more power to Blaylock's swing. His arm completely circled the shorter man's head and wound up coming back straight at Blaylock himself. His fist crunched in his own jaw—sending him reeling against the rope. He managed to stand for a few seconds, groggily trying to stay upright. But then he collapsed and was counted out.

He had knocked himself out.

☞ **L** ☜

ON LECTURES, ODD:

Noted British journalist Auberon Waugh was accustomed to receiving lecture invitations, but this one seemed a little odd: A Senegalese magazine had invited him to go to Dakar to deliver a lecture on breast-feeding.

Breast-feeding? It seemed like an odd topic, since he ordinarily wrote and spoke on political topics. But they were offering him a free trip to Senegal—so he accepted.

He worked feverishly on his speech on this new subject. To be sure he would be understood, he even wrote his speech in French, an official language of Senegal.

He arrived in Senegal at the lecture site and began his speech. It was a "passionate argument against the practice of breast-feeding," as he later recalled in his memoirs.

The audience of journalists, diplomats, and Senegalese officials looked surprised.

It wasn't until later that he learned that the speech topic had somehow gotten garbled in the translation. It wasn't "breast-feeding" he should have been addressing, but "press freedom."

On Legal Decisions:

A court in New York awarded two students from Pratt University $1,000. They had sued the university, claiming the math in their computer course was "too hard."

On Life After Death:

An Israeli hospital patient was heavily sedated for two weeks after receiving kidney and pancreas transplant operations. He was awakened when he heard the sound of a missile alert. When he looked up from his bed, he saw doctors and nurses—all wearing gas masks because of the air-raid threat—surrounding him. His immediate thought: He had died and gone to either heaven or hell.

The surgeon noticed how upset the patient was, removed his gas mask, and tried to reassure the patient that everything was fine. In fact, he told the man, the patient's mother had been by the hospital every day to see how he was.

That was the last straw, as far as the patient was concerned. His mother had passed away four years before. Obviously, then, he was dead.

The surgeon didn't know this, of course. The woman he was referring to was another woman who had been at the hospital with the patient's father.

On Lincoln, Little-Known Words by:

In 1972, a computerized statue of Abraham Lincoln was set up at the Northgate Center in Seattle. The statue was a wonder of modern science. With two thousand computerized parts, it seemed almost real—it breathed like a human, its heart beat like a human's, and out of its mouth came the wise words of the great President—from a speech recorded by a Hollywood actor.

It was as if Lincoln had come back to life.

On the day of the statue's debut to the American public, a large crowd had gathered, all waiting to hear the immortal words of Lincoln's celebrated address—the one that begins with the stirring words: "What is that we hold most dear amongst us? Our own liberty and prosperity. . . ."

The crowd waited as Lincoln began his speech to the American people. In a voice somehow different, yet somehow familiar, the great man began . . .

I wanna tell ya I can hardly speak.
I wanna get off, mamma. . . .

Unbeknownst to the shocked organizers and fans, the Lincoln computer's receivers were picking up a stronger signal from the local rock station, featuring Mick Jagger and the Rolling Stones.

SPECIAL SECTION

LUNATIC LAWS

"The law is a ass—a idiot," says Mr. Bumble in Charles Dickens's *Oliver Twist*.

We find it hard to argue with sentiments like that, although we'd say "an ass" and "an idiot" like we learned in English class. In fact, almost everyone would agree that the law is an ass.

The only people who maybe wouldn't agree would be lawyers and politicians who, after all, are responsible for most laws in the first place.

So why do they make such idiotic laws? Probably because they just can't help it. Lawmakers, any psychiatrist could tell you, are almost obsessive about making laws: "The more, the merrier" seems to be their motto. And if most of the laws are absolutely idiotic, who cares?

After all, there's no law against being stupid . . . yet.

☞ A law added to California's books in 1953 makes it a felony for anyone to possess a blowgun. Possession of a firearm, however, is merely a misdemeanor.

☞ Federal flight regulations in Canada make no bones about it: No one, by law, can enter a Canadian aircraft while it is in flight. The law does not specify how someone could do this in the first place. In addition, no one may legally leave an airplane that is flying, except to make a parachute jump. Those who want to make a parachute jump can't get away from the Canadian federal regulations, either. Jump from an airplane without a parachute in Canada and you're in major trouble—from the police. By law, anyone wanting to make a parachute jump must have a parachute or face federal prosecution.

☞ The Singapore government takes bathroom habits very seriously. In 1989, the government issued a new law levying a $510 fine for people who don't flush the toilet in public restrooms. How to enforce this law? The government cleverly enlisted a crack battalion of inspectors whose only job is to roam the public restrooms of the city and catch culprits in the act of leaving toilets unflushed.

☞ In a related measure, the Singapore government installed special sensors and cameras in elevators in most public housing apartment buildings. If any late-night carouser decides to urinate in the elevator, the sensors detect this, special alarms go off, and the elevator doors automatically shut until police arrive. Needless to say, Singapore has a very low crime rate—and the lowest rate of unauthorized urination in the world.

☞ If you're packing a warhead, stay out of Chico, California. This city has a ban on nuclear weapons—with a $500 fine for anyone setting off a nuclear bomb within city limits.

☞ Texas State Representative Jim Kaster introduced a bill requiring anyone wanting to commit a crime to tell the future victim at least twenty-four hours in advance—and to notify them of the right to use deadly force.

☞ A bill was introduced in Oklahoma requiring men to get advance, *written* permission from any female with whom they have sex. In addition, men would be required to tell women they could get pregnant and that pregnancy could be hazardous to health—introduced by Oklahoma State Representative Cleta Deatherage. In a politically correct touch, she added a requirement that if a female could not read the written warnings, she must be read them in her native language. The bill was defeated.

☞ In 1980, the Wyoming legislature banned the photographing of rabbits from January through April without written permission.

☞ An antibigotry resolution in Walworth County, Wisconsin, in the interests of unbiased PC behavior, took out terminology that referred to white supremacist organization like the American Nazis as "hate groups." Instead, they are to be referred to as "unhappy groups."

☞ A bill almost passed by the California State Assembly saluting Yellowstone National Park as one of California's major tourist attractions. One problem: Yellowstone is in Idaho, Montana, and Wyoming.

☞ A Great Britain law makes it illegal for trucks to drive under bridges that are too low for them to drive under.

If you're wondering how stupid laws like the preceding can be written, we have an idea: Maybe the lawyers or legislators responsible attended Bombay Law, an Indian law school that must be turning out some very unusual lawyers. Herewith, to support our hypothesis, are some questions from the LL.B. exam given at the Law School of Bombay University, India, as quoted by *The Times* of India:

☞ "Neccesity knwows no law." Discus.

☞ Distinguish between theft and Exfortion . . . what is defarnation?

☞ A is at work with a batchet: the bead fies off and kills a man who is standing by. HAs A committed any offence?

☞ What is culpasle homicide. When does culpasle homicide amount to murder.

☞ Explain three of the exceptions to the offence of defarnation.

M

ON MERCHANT NAVIES, PECULIAR:

The Swaziland Transport Minister had an uncomfortable moment in Parliament in April of 1994: The landlocked African country had completely lost track of its only ship, the *Swazimar*.

The minister was optimistic, though. "The situation is absolutely under control. Our nation's merchant navy is perfectly safe. We just don't know where it is."

When pressed by a member of Parliament, the Transport Minister tried to be more precise about the whereabouts of the one-ship navy:

"We believe it is at sea somewhere. At one time, we sent a team of men to look for it, but there was a problem with drink, and they failed to find it, and so, technically, yes, we've lost it a bit. But I categorically reject all suggestions of incompetence on the part of this government. The *Swazimar* is a big ship painted in the sort of nice bright colors you can see at night. Mark my words, it will turn up."

ON MIMICS, ROYAL PAINS
WHO ARE:

British biographer Michael Holroyd was at a dinner party with a certain member of the British royal family—who was entertaining the guests with her gift of mimicking different accents.

First she did a North Country accent, then an Irish accent. Then she spoke again.

A little nervous and eager to make a good impression, Holroyd started applauding at the last accent. "Do it again, ma'am," he said, still laughing. "That one's priceless."

Absolute silence. The other dinner guests around the table stared at him in shock. Then it hit him.

She had been speaking in her own voice.

ON MIRACLES,
LESS THAN MIRACULOUS:

Rao was a Hindu yogi, a mystic who devoted his life to prayer and holy thought. And through his discipline he was able to do remarkable things, it was rumored. Finally Rao decided to let the people see him in action. In 1966, he announced that he was going to walk on water. He sent out invitations to six hundred of the cream of Bombay society, charging them as much as $100 a ticket. And the people came, eager to see a miracle with their own eyes.

They weren't disappointed. Rao truly looked like a mystical vision. He stood on the side of a five-foot-deep pond, his beard flowing over his chest, his robes flowing to the ground. He lowered his head in silent prayer, then lifted it. He was ready to walk on water. The crowd leaned forward as he stepped forthrightly over the pond.

Then he sank.

ON MR. PEANUT, WHY HE MAY HAVE SPAWNED THE HUMAN RACE:

Elizabeth Tashijan is a woman with a mission—convincing other people that Darwin, the theorist of evolution, was wrong.

Ms. Tashijan has a different, better theory. Instead of apes, humans evolved from the coco-de-mer, a nut that happens to look a lot like a female's lower torso. The nut is exclusively found in the Seychelles—which some believe was the site of the Garden of Eden. It all came to Ms. Tashijan one day in 1977. She was looking at her favorite coco-de-mer, a thirty-five-pound brute, when she asked herself: "Which was created first? This nut or mortals?" The answer came to her in a flash. As she said, "I became thoroughly convinced that the nut was first."

To spread the word of her theory, she's come up with a snappy slogan: "Out with apes. In with nuts."

And she runs a museum, cleverly called The Nut Museum, out of her home in Old Lyme, Connecticut. The museum is supposed to "establish the entity of nuts through art, music, and lore." It contains more than forty different nuts from around the world. She also has such things as nut paintings, nut jewelry, lawn sculptures with a nut theme, nut masks. She's also written a few songs about nuts, such as "Sweet Nut in a Burr" and the nut anthem, "Nuts Are Beautiful," which opens with the line: "Oh, nobody ever thinks about nuts, nuts can be so beautiful if looked aright."

ON MODERN JAILS, HIGH-TECH VERSIONS:

In January 1982, a new prison opened in Baltimore County, Maryland. It was touted as "the most modern jail in the United States." Virtually escape-proof.

Costing $11.2 million, it was a high-tech wonder: It was computer-controlled, with remote-control cameras panning the building, solar panels to produce the only active solar heating system in a United States detention center.

There were a few bugs, however.

The computer system would periodically go crazy and every so often trap people in different parts of the building.

The remote-control cameras apparently got tired easily. As it was, they could run for only half an hour, then had to be shut down for two hours—or the motors would burn out.

And the environmentally correct solar panels didn't work in the winter. Instead, they froze solid.

Some of the less-high-tech things in the prison didn't work so well, either. Many locks wouldn't lock or, if they could lock, wouldn't open. For some reason, the guardposts were designed so that the guards couldn't see into the cells from them. The microphones used to speak to prisoners were virtually unusable.

So it comes as no surprise to learn that less than three months after it opened, nine prisoners escaped.

How did they do it? Easy. They kicked out one of the unbreakable glass-and-plastic-reinforced windows.

"Don't blame me," the warden said. "I didn't plan this building."

ON MUGGINGS, SURPRISING:

Mrs. Hollis Sharpe was walking her poodle, Jonathan, one night on a Los Angeles street when she was attacked by a mugger, shoved to the ground, and forced to hand over her purse.

No doubt congratulating himself on his easy mugging, the mugger ran off. Unfortunately for the mugger, inside Mrs. Hollis Sharpe's purse was just one item: a plastic bag she had just finished using to scoop up after Jonathan.

ON MUSICAL RECITALS, SWIVELING:

The first rule of inviting a musician to give a piano recital is to make sure the piano works.

Unfortunately, the Erewan Hotel in Bangkok, Thailand, seemed to have more of a "What, me worry?" attitude to piano recitals. This was evident during the early 1970s when the hotel invited a rising young American pianist to give a recital in their chamber music room.

The recital opened without a hitch . . . until the pianist started playing. Only a few minutes into his playing, he noticed the D key of the treble clef kept getting stuck, probably due to the humidity. It was sheer bad luck that he was playing Bach's *Toccata and Fugue in D Minor,* along with his *Prelude and Fugue in D Minor.*

It's tough playing a concert centering on the D key without the D key. The pianist was starting to get rattled.

Things might have gone at least moderately well, but then the problem of the swiveling piano stool intervened. It seemed that one of the hotel workers had greased the swivel on the stool a little too enthusiastically. As the pianist was banging away with a flourish on the keys, he would move slightly, but the overly greased swivel would amplify those movements and periodically whiz him completely around, ripping his hands off the keyboard and turning him to face the audience in midcrescendo.

Getting back to business, the increasingly nervous pianist now decided to abandon all the D minor pieces, sit tight on the stool, and move on to Lizst's *Fantasia in G Minor*. Of course, now it was the turn of the G key in the bass clef to get stuck.

Now the pianist was beginning to lose it.

He kicked the piano with his foot to get the keys unstuck. Of course, one leg of the piano gave away, tilting the piano at an angle of thirty-five degrees.

That was it. The pianist got up, bowed, and, as the audience applauded, walked off the stage.

But he wasn't giving up. Instead, he returned a few seconds later . . . with a fire ax, whereupon he proceeded to attack the piano.

On Name Changes, Logical:

Darryl Wayne Thief was in court, charged with arson. And one of the court officers was cross-examining him, convinced that something fishy was up.

His last name wasn't actually Thief, was it? The officer pressed the accused. Didn't Thief actually have a different last name?

The accused slowly nodded. Yes, he had given a false name, he admitted. But for a good reason. He was actually Darryl Wayne Crook, but he had changed his last name to Thief because Crook gave people the wrong impression.

On NATO Maneuvers, Under the Weather:

In the late 1970s, NATO—the military wing of the U.S.–Western Europe alliance—was all set for White Fox. This was a military exercise to see how the alpine commandos, the elite of the NATO fighting forces, would perform under bad weather conditions.

Then the weather got foggy.

The White Fox exercise was canceled. Why? Bad weather.

ON NICE GUYS FINISHING LAST:

A candidate in a local election in a small town in Poland was a class-act type of guy. To show his respect and his professional courtesy for the candidate running against him, he cast his vote for his opponent.

The problem was, his was the only vote cast out of 595 eligible voters.

ON NORTH AMERICAN GENERALS, DUBIOUS:

In the contest for North America's most inept general, U.S. Generals Burnside and Custer are tied with Mexican General Antonio López de Santa Anna.

Santa Anna idolized Napoleon (even at one time copying his hairstyle), but he never really got Napoleon's tactics and strategy right. Take, for example, Santa Anna's brilliant plan for a super-special surprise attack. Instead of focusing on battle plans, Santa Anna focused on uniforms. Why not, he maintained, put his soldiers into *enemy* uniforms and really give the enemy a surprise?

So the men were dressed in enemy uniforms and launched against the enemy, before someone told Santa Anna the problem with his clever plan. How can you tell who to shoot? Everybody looked alike. The surprise attack ended up as a bloody mess, with Santa Anna's troops managing to shoot more of their own men than the enemy. And so they lost.

O

ON OBITUARIES, EMBARRASSING:

Writer Bret Harte was once working as editor of a small paper in a mining settlement in California. The wife of one of the leading citizens had died, and Harte wrote a glowing obituary. His closing line: "She was distinguished for charity above all the other ladies of this town."

Later on that day he went back to his office to look over the proofs for the next morning's paper. In reading over his obituary, he noticed that the compositor had made a potentially embarrassing typo. Instead of "charity," the compositor had set "chastity." Harte crossed out the *s*, put a large query mark in the margin, and went home, relieved he had caught the error.

The next morning, he turned to the obit and was horrified. It read: "She was distinguished for chastity (?) above all the other ladies of this town."

ON OFFICIAL ANNOUNCEMENTS, AFGHANI-STYLE:

According to a 1978 announcement on Afghanistan's state radio, President Noor Mohammed Taraki resigned "due to ill health."

They didn't elaborate on just what this ill health was—neglecting to say a word about the fact that the President just happened to have twelve bullet holes in his body.

ON THE OLYMPICS, GROUNDBREAKING EVENTS IN:

The World Plowing Association, which sponsors plowing contests for farmers from all over the world, has applied to the Olympic Committee to sponsor plowing contests during the Summer Olympics.

According to a disappointed association spokesperson, "Up to now, we haven't had any reply. I, for one, can't see any real difference between plowing and swimming."

ON OPERA, HAIR-RAISING MOMENTS IN:

The opera *Pelléas et Mélisande,* by Claude Debussy, has a dramatic moment when Mélisande lets down her long plait of hair through a window, under which her lover Pelléas is waiting.

During one production, the opera singer playing Mélisande was wearing a six-foot-long blonde plait and was all set to lower the mass of hair down from the window, where her lover was singing away lustily.

Unfortunately, as she lowered her plaited hair down, her singing lover Pelléas had his mouth open—and his voice died away in a gargling gurgle as mounds of hair filled his mouth.

P

ON PARANOIA:

It was the early 1970s. The Cold War was still being waged and few Westerners had actually been behind the Iron Curtain. But in the interest of sportsmanship, the Soviet Union decided to invite a team of North American ice hockey players to play the Soviet team.

The North American team accepted, but team members were wary of what to expect behind the Iron Curtain. Their guard was up from the minute they arrived in Moscow. And when they were taken to their assigned hotel room, they became convinced that the room must be bugged. Phil Esposito, one of the hockey players, and his teammates had seen the spy movies. They knew that there had to be a microphone concealed somewhere in the room. The question was where.

Talking as normally as possible, they began carefully searching the room. No luck. The room appeared to be clean. Then one of them hit paydirt. There it was—as Esposito described it, "a funny-looking round piece of metal imbedded on the floor, under the rug." It had to be the bug. What else could it be? They dug it out of the floor, proud to have outsmarted their hosts. Then came a crash from the floor beneath them.

They had unscrewed the anchor to the chandelier in the ceiling below.

On Party Preparations:

A Houston couple was throwing a very special party for the crème de la crème of society. The two sent out invitations for, as they called it, a "Secret Dinner" with a special guest of honor: visiting tenor Luciano Pavarotti.

They were so busy setting up their exclusive wingding that they didn't get around to inviting the guest of honor until the last minute. Hours before the dinner was to take place, they finally invited Pavarotti.

He said no.

On the Phone Company, Great Anal-Retentive Moments in:

A man called the phone company to get an unlisted phone number. He was given one and went on to ask the representative on the phone about several features of phone company service. Just as he was about to hang up, he realized he had forgotten his new unlisted number. He asked the phone company representative to repeat the number to him.

"I'm sorry," she said, "I can't. That's an unlisted number."

ON PIG SLAUGHTERING, STUPID INNOVATIONS IN:

A Romanian man had to slaughter his pig, Googo. But he was too squeamish to do this in the normal way, so instead he decided to electrocute the unlucky animal. He wired a mat of chicken wire to the local power line, figuring that the pig would eventually walk over the mat and be electrocuted. The end result would be a clean, simple, safe slaughtering job.

He and his wife waited. And finally Googo, the pig, walked over the mat. The electrical charge was so intense, the pig shot ten feet up into the air. The man ran over to see what was happening, and the pig landed on him, knocking him out. His wife ran over to revive him. In the meantime, the pig ran off and wasn't seen again.

ON PLASTIC BAG DISGUISES, PART 1:

R. V. Dartnell of De Ridder, Louisiana, was foiled in his robbery attempt because he forgot to cut eyeholes in the plastic garbage bag he wore as a disguise.

On Plastic Bag Disguises, Part 2:

Bob Coleman had a slightly different problem. He could see through *his* plastic bag disguise . . .

But so could everyone else. He wore a transparent plastic bag over his head.

On Plastic Bag Disguises, Part 3:

The man holding up patrons at Johnson's Jump bar wore a plastic bag over his head as a disguise . . . but he didn't get the eyehole part right. He cut them so large, everyone could easily see his face.

He was one of the regulars.

After he was let out on bail for this attempt, he couldn't leave well enough alone. He went back to Johnson's and did it again. The bag had smaller eyeholes . . . but this time the bag slipped completely off his head.

ON PLIABLE PEOPLE, PIPES AND:

An excited audience was watching Jonathan Jones, a circus contortionist, go through his act.

A low drumroll announced the climax of the act. Jones was lowered by trapeze over a narrow two-foot-wide pipe. As the announcer explained in a hushed voice, Jones would twist and contort his body and squeeze himself all the way through five feet of the narrow pipe.

As the trapeze lifted away, the audience watched as Jones lowered himself down the pipe, lower and lower, until only his head and part of his chest were sticking out.

The audience watched, and kept on watching, as the head and chest in the pipe shifted and contorted, but stayed put. Finally, after a few minutes, a few laughs broke out, then more and more, as Jones contorted himself over and over, puffing, getting redder and redder in the face. But he didn't manage to move either up or down.

Finally, over the loud din of laughter, someone heard Jones shouting, "You fools, can't you see I'm stuck!"

The man and pipe were together carried to an ambulance and taken to a local emergency room, where Jones was finally extricated after a generous amount of liquid soap was poured into the empty side of the pipe.

ON POETRY READINGS, STUPID:

A poetry reading organized by the Women for Mental Health and Women in a Violent World in 1991 in Canada erupted into violence when a woman began reading the immortal poem "Tampon: An Elegy to the Anti-Clitoral Nature of White Feminism."

Objecting to the poem, a woman from the States for Women Group tried to seize the microphone. Others began shouting in support, and still others, called the Healers, began chanting, "Heart! Heart!"—which supposedly was a peace call to pure individuals.

This annoyed still other feminist poets, and ultimately fighting broke out among poets of all stripes and the police were called in. They arrested ten of the fighting feminist poets.

According to a spokesperson for the group: "This reading indicates that a new level of sophistication has been reached by the women's movement."

ON POLICE LINEUPS, WHAT NOT TO SAY IN:

A bank had been robbed in Glasgow, Scotland, and the police had arrested Robert Dylan. Along with some other men who weren't suspects, he was herded into a police lineup to see if any witness would pick him out. But as Dylan stood there, not one witness identified him as the robber.

All seemed to be going great for Dylan—until he called out: "Hey, don't you recognize me?"

ON POLITICAL CORRECTNESS, GREAT MOMENTS IN:

In 1995, a bill in the Mississippi legislature made caning a legal punishment for criminals.

But legislators realized there might be a bit of a public relations problem with the bill. Their largest concern: Would it cause racial strife? How would people react at the image of white guards caning black prisoners or blacks caning whites?

The farsighted sponsor of the bill, though, had the perfect solution.

The job of caning would be given over to Native Americans.

ON POLITICIANS, SMOOTH:

Geoffrey Dickens, a member of the British Parliament, couldn't shake the attentions of one particular constituent while he was at a local fair. It was a bit irritating: Here he was, pressing the flesh and mingling with his public, and this besotted, unattractive young woman continually followed him around wherever he went.

But his irritation vanished a few days later when he received a letter from her requesting a signed photograph of him. After the signature on her letter, she had written: "(Horseface)." This touch moved him. The poor woman obviously knew her drawbacks, yet had the unassuming sense of humor to deal with them.

So he sent her the photo she requested—being sure to add the personal touch in the form of an inscription: "To Horseface, with best wishes, Geoffrey Dickens."

The photo was sent off and Dickens felt he had done his bit to maintain good relations with his public.

But he got a shock when his secretary later approached him and asked if he had replied to the letter. "It was from the woman at the fair," helpfully added the secretary.

Then he added, "I wrote 'Horseface' after her name so you'd know which one she was."

On Post Office Excuses, Bizarre:

Maybe it only happens in Great Britain. Maybe it's something about British paper, or maybe the post office boxes are oddly located. . . .

Anyway, we submit the following for your approval, two incidents of postal service from the Twilight Zone.

One British woman, Doris Honeysett, received a ragged, torn, and dirty letter in the mail. Attached to it was a brief note from the post office explaining why it was such a mess: It had been eaten by snails.

In another British postal mishap, someone wrote a letter to *The Times* complaining about the post office. The complaint? A mangled letter was returned from Windsor with the note: "Eaten by swans."

ON POTATO THIEVES, BLUNDERS MADE BY:

Maybe potato thieves are dumber than the average run of thieves. Edgar Lunden was easily caught and arrested after stealing six pounds of potatoes from a supermarket. One reason for his easy apprehension? Edgar Lunden had his full name tattooed across his forehead.

But Lunden was a little surprised by his quick arrest: "I did not think anyone would be able to identify me because I do my own tattooing, and as I used a mirror for my forehead, I got the lettering back to front."

ON THE POWER OF THOUGHT, THEORIES ON:

A twenty-two-year-old Chinese man was convinced he had mastered the powers of his mind. Through his superior control of his thoughts, he believed he could cause things to happen—or not to happen.

The key, of course, was putting his theory to a test.

So he stood on a railroad track near Shanghai and applied his thoughts to a speeding train coming right at him. If his theory was correct, he could force the train to stop.

His theory was incorrect.

ON PREGNANCY, BAD WAYS TO PREVENT:

In 1983, China launched an extensive twelve-month program that was carefully designed to teach the fundamentals of birth control to the rural populace. Doctors and nurses were televised demonstrating the use of condoms and birth control pills. People were exhorted to faithfully practice the techniques.

But a scant year later the Chinese minister declared the program a "complete fiasco." The birth rate had actually *increased*.

Experts were puzzled . . . until a survey was conducted. It

showed that most Chinese in the hinterlands were faithfully following birth control techniques: 79 percent of the men were taking the pill every day, and 98 percent of them were carefully putting a condom on their index fingers before sex—just as demonstrated on TV.

ON PRISONS, INMATES PICK THEIR FAVORITE:

Alcoentre Prison, near Lisbon, Portugal, is the world's worst maximum security prison—unless you're an inmate. . . .

In July 1978, prison guards noticed that attendance was down at the nightly film shows. They also happened to notice that over two hundred knives were missing from prison storerooms—as well as electric cables, spades, chisels, water hoses, and drills.

In the immortal words of one guard: "We were planning to look for them, but we never got around to it."

It was too bad they hadn't. Over half of the inmate population used the tools to escape from the prison one night.

But the guards didn't notice that, either.

At roll call, when fewer than half of the prisoners showed up, lackadaisical guards didn't sound the alarm. They just assumed prisoners were hiding somewhere in the prison—something they often did. There happened to be huge holes in the prison walls, but somehow the guards overlooked them as well. They later explained that the holes were difficult to see because they had been covered by posters and, besides, the searchlights were so bright they often blinded the guards' eyes. In fact, the guards didn't "discover" the breakout until the next morning.

How did they finally find out? One of the prisoners told them.

The guards weren't in too much trouble, however, judging from the attitude of their supreme boss. The Portuguese Justice Minister called the escape "normal" and said it was due to the "legitimate desire of the prisoner to regain his liberty."

ON PRODUCT PROMOTIONS THAT GIVE ONE FOOD FOR THOUGHT:

The Rival dog food company had come up with a new product—an all-beef dinner for dogs. And their public relations company, Harshe & Rotman, Inc., had the perfect way to promote the food. They would invite the press to special luncheon. Sitting at the main table as guests of honor? The president of Rival dog food and his special guest, a pedigreed collie—who, the head of the PR firm was told, was well-trained and would be very hungry.

But the worst happened. The press attended the luncheon, ready to get shots of the collie devouring the dog food. But the dog wouldn't bite. He wouldn't even sniff his dish. Desperate to save the moment and to plug the new dog food, the president of Rival finally took the dog's bowl and ate the new all-beef dinner himself.

It worked. The reporters loved it. And the next day the event was in the media, just as the PR company had promised. But the publicity wasn't what Rival president had bargained for. As one headline blared: RIVAL PRESIDENT EATS DOG FOOD, BUT DOG WON'T.

ON PROFESSORS, CRITICAL:

The editors of the Encyclopaedia Britannica contacted the head of a major Western university history department. They sent him a historical article that had been in the encyclopedia for years and asked him if he would be interested in revising it.

The professor promptly sent the article back with a biting note, turning down the request and commenting that the article was "inaccurate . . . badly disorganized and full of errors."

At this point, the editors wondered who had written such a weak article. They went through their files and came up with the name—it had been written by the professor himself, many years before.

ON PSYCHOTHERAPY, PRESSING NEEDS FOR:

Pierre Beaumard was a nervous Frenchman who just couldn't communicate well with others. He also had obsessional fears and complexes.

His therapist thought he had an answer. It was a bit unconventional, but it would work. He put Beaumard between two mattresses, and got four participants from the therapy group to walk on the mattresses, helping to "stamp out" Beaumard's obsessions.

The cure worked. When the top mattress was removed, Beaumard had no complexes to speak of. He was dead of suffocation.

R

ON RACETRACK RESCUES, DEATH-DEFYING:

The Smoky Mountain Raceway ambulance happened to be a reconditioned hearse. And, as one race car driver discovered, its initial use may have been a bad omen.

In 1968, during a race at the Smoky Mountain Raceway, near Maryville, Tennessee, driver Buddy Baker's car blew a tire. The Dodge spun out of control, and at the first turn, slammed into a cement wall. Baker was alive—but badly hurt.

The raceway ambulance sped onto the track to help the injured driver. The medics got out, carefully lifted Baker onto a wheeled stretcher, loaded him into the back of the hearse, and slammed the door.

Unfortunately, the medics didn't *latch* the door.

When the driver hit the gas to quickly get away, the door flew open, and Baker zoomed onto the track, strapped to his gurney.

The speeding gurney kept moving, making its way to the straightaway. And the panicking Baker could see all the other race cars, still driving under the yellow caution flag, headed right for him.

Don Naman, the driver of the pace car that led the field, noticed Baker on the runaway gurney just ahead of him. He motioned the cars behind him to drive as close to the wall as possible, and they all watched as Baker sped past them on the stretcher, closely followed by the ambulance crew.

But it still wasn't over.

The hapless ambulance crew finally caught up to Baker and wheeled him back to the hearse, but this time he refused to go in the back—instead he rode on the front seat alongside the driver.

Bad move. From this vantage point, Baker could see just what was going on. The driver ran a red light, and another car pulled out in front of them. The hearse managed to swerve to miss the car, but it wound up on the sidewalk, where it skidded into a group of garbage cans. Finally the hearse made it to the hospital—with a flat tire and almost no brakes.

Baker said that after he was treated, the ambulance crew offered to drive him back.

"I told them, 'Never mind. I'll find another ride.' "

ON RADAR GUNS, ZIPPY:

A woman was charged with speeding by the police. But she was convinced she hadn't been speeding at all.

When she appeared before the court, she said that she didn't trust the radar gun the police were using when they caught her. She then suggested that the radar gun that recorded her speed be brought to court and tested.

It was.

It was pointed at the judge sitting at the bench and recorded him as traveling at 122 miles per hour.

On Radio, Confusing Moments in:

King George VI and his wife Queen Elizabeth were making a trip across Canada in 1939. Wherever they went, radio broadcasters followed their every move.

In Winnipeg, the royal couple was greeted by the Canadian Prime Minister, MacKenzie King. They were also greeted by the mayor of Winnipeg and his wife—Mr. and Mrs. Queen.

The Canadian Broadcasting Corporation announcer had his work cut out for him doing a coherent on-the-spot report:

"Here comes the royal family now. The automobile has now stopped, a member of the RCMP is opening the car door—oh, there's the King—he's stepping out, followed by Her Majesty Queen Elizabeth, nattily attired in a silver coat. Mr. King is now shaking hands with the King and introducing Mr. Queen to the King and Queen and then Mrs. Queen to the Queen and King. They are now proceeding up the steps to the well-decorated City Hall, the King and Mr. King together, with the Queen being escorted by Mrs. Queen. The King has now stopped and said something to Mrs. Queen and goes to Mrs. Queen and the Queen and Mr. King and the Queen laughed jovially. The King leaves Mr. King and goes to Mrs. Queen and the Queen and Mr. King follow behind. . . ."

On Rescues by the Highway Patrol, Great Moments:

The average Californian must love animals—or so it seemed when a stray puppy wandered onto the Harbor Freeway during rush hour. Traffic slowed to a standstill as anxious drivers tried to avoid a frantic little dog panicked by the bewildering maze of cars. Concerned motorists began backing up their cars, trying to create a path for the dog. To no avail. The puppy was still stuck in the middle of a traffic snarl.

So dog lovers were relieved when the California Highway Patrol appeared on the scene to take charge of the situation. The problem was solved in a jiffy by the efficient officers.

The Highway Patrol squad car pulled up and promptly ran over the dog.

On Rescues by the Military, Great Moments:

During a firemen's strike in 1978, the British Army took over the normal duties of firemen. And typically, one cold January day, they were called by a little old lady to rescue her cat, stuck high in a tree. The Army accomplished its mission quickly and efficiently. The cat came down and the thankful little old lady invited the soldiers in for tea.

Afterward, full of tea and cookies, the soldiers waved good-bye— and ran over the cat.

On Rescues, How Not to Conduct:

A man was out hunting in Arizona when he accidentally shot himself in the leg. Keeping his head about him, he realized that the best way to get help would be to alert other hunters in the area—so he fired his gun again to attract attention.

Unfortunately, he shot himself in the other leg.

On Restaurant Service, Complaining to the Manager About:

A customer at a well-known restaurant, which shall remain nameless, was angry. The chicken on his plate was underdone. He called over the waiter to complain, but the waiter insisted that the chicken looked just fine to him. Next, the customer asked to see the manager. So the manager came over to the table.

Ah, now he would get satisfaction, thought the customer.

The manager picked up the chicken. He took a bite from it . . . then took yet another bite. Finally he put it back on the man's plate.

"Perfect," he said. "A lot better than you get at home."

On Restaurants, Attention-Grabbing:

Any self-respecting businessperson knows that image counts for a lot when it comes to attracting customers.

And Kim Chung-Hee, an enterprising South Korean business-man, was no exception. He was going to open a new restaurant/beer parlor and wanted to be sure to attract the large amount of tourists in South Korea. Since so many of the tourists were Europeans, specifically Germans, he thought long and hard about what would grab their attention. He specifically wanted a name with "an authentic European ring," as he put it.

It wasn't easy. Kim described himself as being no student of history. But finally he came up with the perfect attention-grabbing name.

The Hitler.

He even bought a number of swastika flags to hang on the walls. "Korea guarantees liberty of expression to its people," he said.

Shortly after his restaurant opened, however, the mayor of Seoul asked him to change the name to "something less controversial."

SPECIAL SECTION

SCIENCE GOES STUPID

Einstein working through abstruse mathematical formulas to arrive at relativity, Watson and Crick painstakingly figuring out the helical structure of DNA, Max Planck elucidating the uncertainty of the universe with his formulation of quantum mechanics. . . .

From our perspective, so what?

Yes, these were great moments of human achievement, but did they make anyone laugh?

In compiling this section, we avoided like the plague the great triumphs by the greatest minds in history.

We were on the lookout for littler minds. Bush league scientists, to use a sports metaphor. Or, if you prefer TV metaphors and look at life like a great television schedule in the sky, we were on the lookout for the cheap sitcom reruns instead of *Masterpiece Theatre.*

We wanted the kind of science that swallows grant money or taxpayers' dollars and, at the end of it all, doesn't advance humankind one bit—or maybe even regresses us all a notch or two.

But this kind of science gets a laugh or two. And if you're a hardworking taxpayer, maybe you too can laugh when you realize where some of *your* hard-earned money is going.

☞ In 1990, researchers at the University of Wisconsin–Madison embarked on a scientific study of rhinotillexomania—better known as nose-picking. They mailed out questionnaires to twelve hundred people—containing such deep questions as "What finger do you use when picking your nose?" and "After picking your nose, how often do you find yourself looking at what you have removed?"

☞ In 1982, a sociology professor at the University of Wisconsin, Dr. Ray Short, appeared before a congressional hearing to report on his research into teenage sex. Among his findings: The threat of nuclear holocaust was one of the key reasons why teenagers engaged in sex. Fearing the world might be destroyed by nuclear weapons, teenagers believed that if they didn't have sex when they were young, they might never have the chance to experience it at all.

☞ A British governmental committee needed a definitive ruling on when winter begins and when it ends—so they turned to the Meteorological Office in Bracknell. The scientific reply: "Winter begins when all the leaves have fallen off the trees. And it ends when the bulbs start coming up again."

☞ In late 1994, Utah State University got a whopping $500,000 research grant from the Environmental Protection Agency—to study bovine flatulence. The researchers will round up rangeland cattle and fit them with special breathing devices—to measure just how much methane cows release when they burp. This isn't the only study of this kind. In fact, this Utah State study will expand on a previous bovine flatulence study (a mere $300,000 one) begun in 1991 by Washington State University, which, to quote an Associated Press story, "provoked widespread ridicule."

☞ Psychobiologist Harman Peeke of the University of California at San Francisco ran a $102,000 research study funded by taxpayers' dollars to answer the burning question: Are sunfish that drink tequila more aggressive than sunfish that drink gin? (For his efforts, he won Senator William Proxmire's Golden Fleece award for wasting taxpayers' dollars—which cost him his federal grant and forced him to drop his project.)

☞ Another Golden Fleece award went to the National Institute of Mental Health for funding a $97,000 study of ethnicity in the highlands of Peru. The anthropologists were researching relationships between Indians and mestizos (mixed-blood Indians) in the Peruvian Andes—and as part of their research, investigated a Peruvian brothel to, as the research article put it, "obtain a good idea of its everyday functioning." One researcher, Dr. Pierre L. van der Berghe of the University of Washington, defended himself by saying it was only one aspect of the study. Moreover, he said, it was his research associate Dr. George Primov's idea to write about the brothel. Furthermore, it only cost about $50 and it was "something he did mostly in the evenings."

☞ Jon Erik Beckjord, Bigfoot authority and director of the Crypto-Phenomena Museum in Malibu, California, made a shocking discovery in 1991 after analyzing NASA photographs of Mars. He announced that he discovered a 3.6-mile-wide rock formation that resembles the face of Massachusetts Senator Ted Kennedy. The formation consists of "a volcano, the crater of which gives the impression of a square face, with jowls, fat jowls, a chin protruding out of the jowls. This is a characteristic look of Kennedy.

"This is serious," he added. "This is not a joke."

☞ Dr. E. E. Burns of Texas A&M University discovered a *good* use for nuclear waste. It can be used as a food preservative. The bad news? While the food is preserved, it's also extremely smelly. "For example," explained Burns, "angel food cake with irradiated egg whites smells like a wet dog on a rainy day."

☞ Reverse Speech Technology has been involved in research probing "reverse speech." More precisely, this group holds that when you play recorded speech backward you can discover unconscious "reverse" messages that the speakers are masking—not "Paul is dead," but such insightful words as these uncovered by playing back CNN reporter John Holliman during his Gulf War coverage.

His on-air statement: "The antiaircraft fire is now going to the south. We're looking out to the west and we see the tracer bullets going."

This, played backward, revealed the following hidden message: "To hell with it. The bastards don't know it's Fonzie. Don't tell them it's yesterday."

☞ A professor of animal psychology at the University of Alberta conducted a five-year research project concerning sheep that stemmed from a seminar on ductile intelligence parameters. In simpler English, she and her students were attempting to teach sheep weight lifting. She developed a vest with pockets that could be put on the sheep. Weights were slipped into the pockets before the sheep began grazing. But the vests turned out to be a failure, and the professor abandoned the project. Her conclusion? Sheep had motivation problems.

☞ One professor decided to turn his research into a moneymaking enterprise. Dr. Terence Glanville studied wood lice at the University of Nottingham—and came up with a great idea: wood lice racing. He designed a ten-lane wood lice track upon which lice with numbers painted on their backs could race. To make it even more exciting, people could cover the course with a damp cloth, which increased the speed of the lice. Back in 1984, Glanville was convinced he was onto something huge. "I am convinced wood lice racing will take off in a big way." We're still waiting.

☞ The *Journal of Clinical Psychology* published the results of a research study conducted by five California psychologists in 1987. The subject of this groundbreaking study? Body-elimination attitude and vocational interest or, in simpler language, what people with different college majors think about going to bathroom.

Among their findings: "Students with business-oriented majors expressed more body-elimination disgust than those with human-services-oriented majors. On the Thurstone Interest Inventory, the Business scale was associated positively with disgust, and the Humanitarian and Linguistic scales were associated negatively with this aversion."

☞ Biologists at the University of California–Irvine conducted yet another groundbreaking study: on snake locomotion. The biologists strapped snake-size oxygen masks on the snakes they were studying and watched them as the snakes crawled on treadmills. The conclusion: A not-so-surprising observation that snakes, lacking legs or feet and shaped like cylinders, can fit into small openings.

☞ A study at the Royal University of Stockholm, Sweden, found that old people move their legs with greater speed when they are in a hurry.

☞ Most people eat lunch because they are hungry. This finding was "revealed" from a study done by Taiwan's Council for Agricultural Planning and Development. The study also found that other people ate lunch because they like to eat three meals a day, and lunch was one of the three meals.

☞ An earth-shattering study by Dr. Norris Thomson has found that people who don't go to the doctor much don't go because they aren't sick.

S

ON SAFETY DEMONSTRATIONS:

William Michini was an ex-Philadelphia fireman with a point to prove. He had been fired for having long hair—which the fire department claimed was a safety threat.

Michini decided not to take his dismissal sitting down. Instead, he took his case to federal court.

In court, he argued that his hair didn't interfere with his duties. It wasn't unsafe at all. In fact, he claimed, hair couldn't burn. It was self-extinguishing. To demonstrate his claim, he confidently struck a match and held it to his head.

He set his head on fire.

ON SCOTTISH MOUNTAIN-CLIMBING FEATS:

Mr. Kenneth Campbell of Sutherland, Scotland, had a dream. To ascend to the peak of Ben Nevis in Scotland—dragging a 250-pound organ.

His first noble attempt failed, probably due to the wrong choice of instrument. He was pushing a grand piano up Ben Nevis when the piano crashed over a low cliff and dragged Campbell a hundred feet after it.

Undaunted, Campbell returned home, hitched himself to an organ, and vowed to try again. He started immediately. His routine was simple. He would pull the organ a mile or two, then set up camp at night. Each morning after awakening, he would eat some porridge, then play a resounding chorus of "These Are My Mountains" and set on his way. The *Glasgow Herald* in 1971 reported him well above the snowline, organ in hand.

It was all for a good cause. "I'm doing it all to aid cancer research," Campbell said.

ON SELF-HELP MEETINGS, NOT-SO-HELPFUL:

Some people just can't help being a little anxious. This is probably why self-help books and courses are so popular—and why Alan Black of the Nottingham Health Authority decided to hold a course at a local school.

His course was called "Why Worry?" and was intended to give antianxiety lessons to (presumably) anxious participants. Ten people showed up for the first class, and Black started in on his anxiety-combatting lessons.

Possibly the course content was marvelous—but probably anxiety levels rose instead of fell when the class ended. An overzealous janitor going about his nightly rounds locked the school as he usually did.

Unfortunately, all ten participants plus the instructor were accidentally locked in the building overnight.

ON SEPARATION CELEBRATIONS, BANG-UP:

Cesar de Mana, a Brazilian fisherman, was a happy man. After some not-so-blissful wedded years, his wife had finally agreed to a separation. So the newly freed de Mana invited three women over for a festive dinner—which he would cook himself. It was time for a real bang-up celebration—and that's just what de Mana got.

The wine flowed, and de Mana and friends became cheerfully drunk . . . and hungry. So the slightly sodden de Mana went into the kitchen to cook his specialty—sausages. He grabbed four of them, tossed them in the pan, and began frying.

A split second later, the kitchen—in fact, the entire house—blew up. He and his guests wound up the celebration by staying in the hospital.

He had thrown four sticks of dynamite into the frying pan by mistake.

On Shark Attacks, Why Your Public Relations Expert Knows Best:

Beachgoers at the town of South Padre Island, Texas, were beginning to go into a panic. Everyone was whispering about it: "Sharks! Don't go in the water!"

The word was spreading that two women had been bitten by sharks while swimming at the beach.

Not to worry, said town spokesman Joe Rubio. It wasn't a shark attack, but a shark *accident*. "More than likely he ran into her leg and got it caught in his mouth."

On Short Story Competitions, Not Open to PEN Members:

The government of Iran announced a short story competition in 1994. A first prize of ten gold coins would be awarded to the story that best depicts the "moments of fear and anxiety" that British author Salman Rushdie experienced after the Ayatollah Khomeini issued an edict calling on Muslims to kill him.

The winner has not yet been announced.

ON SMALL TALK, DISASTROUS:

An English aristocrat was sitting in a box next to Lord North and started a conversation with him. He noticed two women walk into the box directly opposite and chose it as a topic of conversation.

"Who is that ugly woman who just came in?"

Lord North smiled. "Oh, that is my wife," he said pointedly.

His companion grew flustered. "Sir, I beg your pardon. I do not mean her. I mean that shocking monster who is along with her."

"That," replied Lord North, "is my daughter."

ON THE SPACE RACE, INTERESTING WAYS TO KEEP UP WITH:

It was the early days of the space race and Zambia wasn't going to be left out of the running. In fact, Minister of Space Nkoloso confidently announced that Zambia would soon have a man on the moon. No matter that Zambia didn't have quite the technical expertise or the money to support programs like those in the United States and Soviet Union. They would make do with what they had.

And that's just what they did. The Zambian government got the program up and running. Proud of their achievement, they invited reporters to see the different aspects of the Zambian space program—

which gave credence to the old saying "Where there's a will, there's a way."

Why be held back by the lack of high-tech equipment? To simulate the effects of orbital flight, the Zambians rigged up their own noncomputerized version: A future astronaut would curl up in a barrel that was attached to a tree by a rope. Assistants would then whirl the barrel around the tree.

In another low-tech, nonscientific touch, future astronauts were being trained to walk on their hands—"the only way humans can walk on the moon," as the Space Minister asserted.

To date, they still haven't gotten a man on the moon.

On Spies, Crackerjack:

It was 1975 and the Basque separatist movement in Spain had everyone on tenterhooks. There had been terrorist bombings, threats of further violence, and the like.

In the midst of this tension, two undercover agents from the Civil Guard were on duty in Vitoria. They noticed three suspicious-looking men and began covertly following them from the evening well into the night. When the three suspects entered a Basque nightclub at midnight, the undercover agents were more convinced than ever that their hunch was right and followed them in. It was time to trap their prey.

They saw the men sitting in a corner, but when they marched over, prepared to arrest them, the three men turned the tables. They jumped up, grabbed the unsuspecting agents, pulled the agent's arms behind their backs, and pushed them out of the building.

The three "terrorists" explained that they were undercover agents, working for the Civil Guard, who had been tailing the other two men—because they looked suspicious.

ON STAGE SETS, EXCESSIVE:

Too much of almost anything is not good. This elementary idea had evidently not hit the brain of the set designer of the play *Intimate Review,* which opened on March 11, 1930.

Simply put, he had cluttered the stage with so much scenery and so many props that it took over twenty minutes to change sets. In the words of the critic for *The Times* of London, this meant that the audience kept getting "glimpses of things we were not meant to. Every time the curtains parted, squads of scene-shifters might be seen in action or in horrid precipitate flight."

The first time this happened, the audience took it in stride. A simple mistake, they thought. But the play went on. Each time the scenes changed and the curtain went up, the audience would be greeted by panicky stagehands scuttling about like roaches caught out in the open, frantically trying to move mountains of scenery and knickknacks.

And each time this happened, the audience laughed a little more loudly, a little more hysterically.

Then Florence McHugh came onstage. Dressed in "native" costume, she began singing "Hawaiian Idyll." This was bad enough—but, of course, the stagehands were still busily moving scenery while she sang. Behind Florence McHugh, the audience could see stagehands wrestling with two sea monsters behind an unfortunately transparent backdrop. It ruined the idyllic Hawaiian atmosphere irretrievably.

At this point, in the interests of damage control, the play's director decided to cut to the finale.

And here the costume designer revealed himself to be a genius on par with the set designer. Six dancers were supposed to appear in the guise of Greek nymphs, flitting back and forth across the stage. The problem was that their headpieces were so enormous that the nymphs lumbered across the stage instead, tottering with the unwieldy weight on their heads. Worse yet, two nymphs then got their headpieces caught together. While three of the other nymphs clustered around, trying to disentangle the two, only the sixth nymph, staunch Florence McHugh of "Hawaiian Idyll" fame, was left to bravely sing the closing song as the hysterical audience howled with laughter.

The show closed the next day. In a masterpiece of understatement, the producers said, "In regard to the accommodation onstage, there was certainly the appearance of overcrowding." They promised to practice some more and reopen later in the year.

ON STOCK MARKET MOVES, STUPID:

The grandfather of 1940s movie star Lana Turner was an early major investor in a struggling soft drink company called Coca-Cola.

The drink tasted good enough, the grandfather reasoned. But he wasn't completely sure about his investment. He became convinced that that awful name was going to kill sales.

He sold out and put the money into a more promising corporation, one that had a product which he *knew* would take the world by storm: the Raspberry Cola Company.

ON STUPID WAYS OF PRETENDING YOU KNOW WHO YOU'RE TALKING TO:

Mrs. Richard Harding Davis, a socially prominent woman, was traveling on the Long Island Rail Road when another woman approached her. It was wonderful to see her again, the woman said. It had been too long!

During the niceties, Mrs. Davis desperately tried to remember who this stranger was. The face was familiar, but she drew a blank when it came to the woman's name.

Oblivious to the fact that Mrs. Davis didn't remember her, the second woman went on talking. Then Mrs. Davis thought she might have found a way out of the predicament, when her unknown companion mentioned her brother.

"Your brother," Mrs. Davis said eagerly. "Of course, I couldn't forget your brother. And what is he doing now?"

Her companion looked at her oddly. "My brother," she—Mrs. Douglas Robinson, sister of Teddy Roosevelt—said, "is still President of the United States."

On Suicide Attempts:

Two Sheffield, England, police officers saw a man sitting in his car with a hose in his mouth. The other end of the hose was attached to the exhaust. The officers sprang into action.

They rushed over, managed to open the locked door, carried the man out to their patrol car, and drove him to the hospital. Two days later, the man made a full recovery. And on his way home, the would-be suicide made sure to stop at the police station to speak to his rescuers.

He demanded a full inquiry into how the officers had scratched the paintwork on his car.

On Suicide Hotlines, Suicidal:

In New York City back in 1980, a woman married to a dentist decided to end it all. Hesitating before actually killing herself, she called a suicide hotline and told the hotline operator of her despair. At the end of it all, the operator said, "Go right ahead. It will be one less mouth to feed." He then hung up.

The woman told a neighbor, who told her she had had the same experience, and had been told to "drop dead." The two then decided to check out the hotline one more time, and called the number. This time they got a new reply: "Call back tomorrow. I'm tired. I want to sleep."

That did it. As the woman explained, "I found my husband's gun, went to the address given in the telephone book, and shot the man dead."

On Sunglasses, Super-Duper:

Back in the days of communism, a Ukrainian factory manufactured sunglasses that worked . . . a little too well. Not only did they keep out the glare, they kept out everything else. People wearing them couldn't see anything at all, even the sun if they looked directly at it. The same factory was also responsible for making plastic footballs that burst like soap bubbles when kicked.

SPECIAL SECTION

STUPID SONGS

You can divide all music, like Caesar did Gaul, into three basic types.

There are the few great pieces. In this case, we don't necessarily mean just the classics, we mean any type of song or piece that deservedly wins a Grammy, the type that you can't get out of your head, the type that somehow makes you cry every time.

Then there's the great majority. The so-so stuff. You don't love it, you don't hate it. You listen. And you forget.

And there's the rare few, the precious few, that are beautifully, unbelievably stupid. Unfortunately, this book isn't multimedia, so we could include the awful music itself. But the stupid lyrics and song titles included here speak for themselves. So, without further ado, here's our collection of stupid songs, a hit parade of hysteria.

☞ Kudos for the longest stupid song title goes to this song, written in 1941: "I'm Looking for a Guy Who Plays Alto and Baritone and Doubles on a Clarinet and Wears a Size Thirty-Seven Suit." It was a hit.

☞ Stacey Hart, the "Saucy Songstress," won National Condom Week's competition for her catchy song—a comedy rap number called "Jiggy, Jiggy, Jiggy—Slip It On!"

☞ "I'm Vasectomized" reached number three on the Thai charts in the early 1980s.

☞ One of the first feminist pop songs was the multicultural "Wigwam Bam." According to a write-up about it in England's *Record Mirror,* it told the "consciousness-raising tale of how squaw Minnehaha shed her culturally determined position of subservience and took on the dominant role of predator with the joyous yell: 'Wigwam bam/gonna make you my man!' "

☞ "The Drunk Driver" by Ferlin Husky is a cautionary country ditty that leaves you weeping. To put it as simply as possible, it's about a husband who, after an intense argument with his wife, goes to drown his sorrows at a nearby bar. When he later drunkenly drives home, he accidentally puts his car into reverse and runs over his own children.

☞ For a truly depressing time, take a listen to the single "Unhappy New Year," released in 1979 and sung (well, actually *talked,* against a background of music) by Steve Dahl. This song takes you, year by year, through a very depressing life. To wit: "In 1974, I lost my left leg in a boating accident. In 1975, well, skip '75 . . . In 1976, I lost my job. . . ." And so it goes, through all the gory details. By the end of the song, he has met the woman of his dreams, lost her to another man, then killed her. He then winds up on Death Row, where, as he explains in the last line, he's going to be electrocuted at one minute before midnight. Happy New Year and end of song.

☞ Points for great song name and lyrics have to go to the not-so-memorable song sung by British singer Melodie Suggs: "You Dun Stomped on My Heart." Wails Suggs, "You dun stomped on my heart/you dun mashed that sucker flat. You dun sorta/stomped on my aorta. . . ."

☞ A 1979 Italian disco chart-topper about Pope John Paul II included the catchy lyrics: "He's the groove, he's the man, that new Pope in the Vatican. . . ."

T

ON TAR PITS,
STICKY SITUATIONS AT:

It was a hot day at the La Brea Tar Pits. An employee got himself into a sticky situation when he noticed a traffic cone that had been tossed into a pit. He tried to retrieve the cone, but wound up getting himself stuck in the tar instead.

He was struggling desperately to free himself, when a man and a child walked by and saw him.

Did they help?

Of course not.

Instead, the man saw fit to use the incident as a compelling reenactment of ancient history. "See?" he told the child. "That's what happened to the dumb animals."

ON TELEPHONE RINGERS, BREAKING THE SOUND BARRIER AND:

Sometimes the phone just doesn't ring loudly enough. So a British eccentric attached his telephone ringer to a set of Klaxon siren bells.

Whenever anyone calls him, the enormously loud Klaxon sounds, literally waking or rousing anyone within a mile of his house.

Angry neighbors brought him to court, but the man was nonplussed. As he put it to the judge: "It has been said that the word 'unreasonable' describes the creation of a Klaxon noise on Sunday morning. However, we are no longer a nation of churchgoers, but of drivers; being awakened by a Klaxon is no different than being awakened by church bells." He added: "As for the six telephone Klaxon calls made one morning last month, that was the work of a peace-and-quiet fanatic whom I saw creeping through the bushes with a decibel meter."

ON TERRORIST GROUPS, NOT-SO-TERRIFYING:

The Gatti Gang was Italy's answer to Joey Gallo's Gang That Couldn't Shoot Straight. The Milan-based cell of the notorious Red Brigade, this gang wasn't as much notorious for its terrorist activities as for its inspired bungling.

Being a terrorist gang requires a number of basic elements. You have to plan terroristic acts; you have to raise the money and then gather the weapons to commit these acts; and you have to commit them. The Gattis typically failed on all three fronts.

First of all, the gang often couldn't hold their important strategy sessions, because Enrico Gatti, their leader, suffered from debilitating colds. When they did manage to strategize, they faced another road-block: When you're a member of a subversive group, you often have to raise money by illegal methods—like robberies. Problem was, none of the twenty-eight Gatti Gang members could drive a car.

But what they lacked in driving ability, they made up for in determination. They took buses everywhere, robbed one bank using a getaway motor scooter, and generally kept plugging. And they were successful . . . marginally. An example of one of their better hauls: 18,000 lira or about $10.

Most terrorist groups also have a decent amount of weapons. But not the Gattis. They had only one bomb for the years when they were theoretically terrorizing the countryside—and they were too scared of the bomb to actually use it. (This prompted another terrorist to tell them to toss in the towel because they were a danger to everyone.) Their guns were so old that they couldn't be fired—so the Gattis tried to replace them, but were taken for $2,000 when the arms deal blew up.

The Gatti Gang went out with as much of an idiotic flair as they conducted business. After ten years, Enrico Gatti finally had enough and gave himself up. He gave an impassioned speech in the courtroom and eloquently urged his followers: "Desert! It's all over. Ten years of struggle have brought us nothing but tears. Lots of our young members want to go home and live in peace."

ON THEME RESTAURANTS, STUPID MOMENTS IN:

It wasn't the most appetizing idea for a restaurant, but Gordon and Jasmine Geisbrecht thought they had a real winner.

In the mid-'70s, they opened a restaurant in Winnipeg, Manitoba, called The Outhouse.

They carried the entire bathroom theme into the interior design. Toilet bowls alternated with tables in the main dining room, and a toilet seat appeared as a logo on all the menus. But the restaurant wasn't a success—chiefly because it was forced to close shortly after opening.

The problem? Not enough *working* bathrooms.

ON THIEVES, NOT-SO-SMART:

In Vang, Norway, a group of professional thieves were carrying out a carefully planned robbery. Everything was going like clockwork.

They broke into a company at night, located the safe, and set up an explosive charge that would just blow the door of the safe off, enabling them to get to the money inside. After setting the fuse, they ran into the next room, crouched behind the wall, and waited for the explosion.

It came a few seconds later. The safe door was blown off. So was the roof. In fact, the entire building collapsed, trapping the robbers, still crouching in the next office, under the rubble.

There had been one problem they hadn't foreseen: Instead of money, the safe had been filled with dynamite.

On Timetables, Useful:

Passengers in the English county of Staffordshire were angry.

The buses on the route from the town of Hanley to Bagnall weren't stopping at bus stops to pick them up.

A bus company official heard their complaints. Yes, it was true, he said. But he had a clear explanation.

If the buses stopped, the timetable wouldn't be accurate.

On Touchdowns, Historic Dumb:

There are two ways to assure that your name will live forever in sports history. One way is to make a spectacular play that leads your team to victory.

This is about the other way.

It's about how Roy Reigels went down in college football history for one particular play in the 1929 Rose Bowl.

A player for the University of California, Reigels recovered a Georgia Tech fumble. California fans went crazy, since Reigels was in great position—only thirty yards from the goal line. Four Georgia

Tech tacklers moved to block his path. Reigels swerved sharply. That's when he saw a clear route to the goal and started sprinting toward it.

Reigels was a center, a position not usually known for the swiftness of its runners. But today Reigels was giving it his all, running as if his life depended on it.

While his running was incredible, his sense of direction wasn't. After he had recovered the ball and evaded his pursuers, he had somehow turned completely around and began a sixty-nine-and-a-half-yard dash toward the *other* goal line. Some of his teammates were equally confused, throwing blocks for him as he ran.

The crowd was stunned; even broadcaster Graham McNamee couldn't figure out what was going on. "What's the matter with me!" he yelled into his mike as Reigels crossed the fifty-yard line. "Am I crazy?"

One of his teammates, Benny Lom, began running after him, but Reigels was unstoppable. "Get away from me!" he yelled at Lom, convinced that Lom was trying to steal his great play. "This is *my* touchdown!" Then at the two-yard line, Lom managed to pull him down. The ball was only six inches from the enemy goal—and Reigels earned the unfortunate nickname Roy "Wrong-Way" Reigels.

California lost the game. But Reigels was famous. His play was written about in over 4,500 feature stories—and took up about 250,000 column inches in sports columns around the country the next day.

ON TOUCHDOWNS, HISTORIC DUMB—RUNNER-UP:

It was a moment that still lives in the annals of college football history. The West Virginia Mountaineers were playing the Rutgers Scarlet Knights in 1922. It was near the end of the second quarter, and Rutgers was being pummeled by the Mountaineers.

There was a Scarlet Knights pileup at the Rutgers forty-three-yard line. A Rutgers defensive player, Bob Dickinson, dove into the pileup and suddenly saw his golden opportunity: The ball popped out of the hands of the Mountaineer running back.

It was Rutgers' chance for scoring. Dickinson got his hands on the ball, tucked his head down, and started charging for the goal line. One tackler hit him, but he kept on running. Then another tackler hit him at the Mountaineers thirty-five-yard line. And still Dickinson kept running—oblivious to the fact that the second tackle had completely spun him around.

He was now running downfield toward his own goal line.

The field ahead was empty. It looked like a clear shot for a touchdown for the Mountaineers.

But then Joe Setron and Charley Howard, two West Virginia players, looked at the empty field, saw their opponent running with the ball, and got a little confused. "Let's get him," one of them yelled, and both took off after Dickinson.

"No, don't!" yelled their teammates, seeing their chances for a touchdown—or, at the least, a safety—dim. So *they* started running after the two Mountaineers . . . who were still running after the Scarlet Knight . . . who was still running toward the wrong goal.

Twenty-five yards later, Setron and Howard finally caught up with Dickinson, tackled him at the Rutgers thirty-two-yard line, and lay there congratulating themselves on their run—until their furious teammates ran over and chewed them out royally.

Finally they realized that they had blown it.

Adding insult to injury, Dickinson, the player who had started the whole mess, had the last word. "Thanks for helping me out," he told his two hapless opponents. "I would have really looked like a fool if I had made it to the end zone. But you guys were even bigger fools for tackling me."

ON TOURIST ATTRACTIONS, HOT IDEAS IN:

The Manchester Parks Department of England came up with an intriguing tourist attraction, glowingly written up in a pamphlet designed to be handed out to visitors.

The attraction? The new city crematorium.

As the handout so catchily put it: "We show you what goes on behind the scenes at a cremation. . . . The furnace will be open and the bone crusher in view. . . . People will be amazed at the cleanliness and hygiene of it all. . . . There is no reason why the whole family should not come. . . . There will be no age limits."

And finally the clincher that the city apparently hoped would turn tourists into potential customers: "Once Dad has been cremated at Blackley, the whole family will follow suit."

Maybe it's something about Great Britain and crematoriums, but another town in Great Britain also opened its crematorium to the public. It was part of Scun-thorpe's twentieth-anniversary celebration.

Over two thousand visitors toured the facility, accompanied by tasteful music on the pipes. Said a spokesman for the health committee: "They have examined bone crushers and have learned how long it takes the ovens to consume an average-sized corpse. Everyone was delighted with what they saw."

ON TOURIST PROMOTIONS, HOTTER IDEAS IN:

In the late 1980s, Ukrainian government officials cooked up a hot tourist idea: offering tours of Chernobyl, the nuclear reactor that blew up in 1986.

Among the sights tourists can see: the city of Chernobyl itself, a radioactive waste dump, and the concrete sarcophagus containing the destroyed reactor.

All visits begin and end with Geiger counter checks of tourists. There's an added tourist benefit: As the newspaper *Komsomolskaya Pravda* reported, anyone needing treatment for radiation exposure will receive it for no additional charge.

And there's even a stop at the town where the radiation workers live. The town's slogan: "Life is good, but too short."

On Tourists, Confused:

Mr. Nicholas Scotti was happy, sitting on the airplane. He was going back to his native country of Italy after years of living in San Francisco.

En route to Italy, the plane made a refueling stop at New York's Kennedy Airport. Mr. Scotti, who didn't speak English too well, misunderstood the words "refueling stop." Thinking he had arrived at his destination, he got off the plane and went into the airport.

His nephews weren't there to meet him, but Mr. Scotti assumed they had been caught in the notorious Roman traffic they had told him about in their letters. So he found his own way out of the airport.

He *was* a little surprised at the great number of changes that had occurred in Italy since he had left—but after all, this was 1977 and it was natural to assume that many old monuments had been destroyed. It was also somewhat surprising to find how many people spoke English, but after all, American tourists were everywhere. Why, the government had even put up street signs in English for their benefit!

But Mr. Scotti didn't have time for speculation. He had some relatives to meet. So he asked a passing police officer in Italian for directions to the bus terminal. The policeman, who by the best of coincidences happened to be from Naples, answered in fluent Italian, and Mr. Scotti followed his directions and found the bus terminal, where he boarded a bus. After many fruitless attempts to understand Mr. Scotti and to help the man find his nephews, the bus driver turned him over to another policeman, who this time didn't speak Italian. This prompted Mr. Scotti to complain out loud about the absurdity of the Italian government, employing policemen who couldn't speak the language.

Finally the mystery was solved—but not for Mr. Scotti. Even when told (in Italian) that he was in the wrong city and the wrong country, Mr. Scotti refused to believe he had been in error. As a police escort sped him back to Kennedy Airport, he pointed at the speeding cars outside the car window and said, "See? I know I'm in Italy. That's how they drive."

ON TOURISTS, OVERLY COMPLIANT:

It was a damp November in 1979, and a group of tourists were sightseeing in the British palace of Westminster.

The Lord Chancellor, Lord Hailsham, was walking across the lobby of the House of Commons, when he spotted his friend, Member of Parliament Neil Marten. Remembering that it was Marten's birthday, Hailsham waved to his friend and yelled out, "Neil!"

At that command, the entire group of tourists immediately fell to their knees in prayer.

ON TRAIN COMPANIES, EXCESSIVE REALISM IN SAFETY STANDARD TESTING AND:

British Rail, the British train system run by the government, decided to lash employees to poles between nine feet and six and a half feet from the tracks, in order to test new safety standards.

A British Rail spokesperson commented, "We could do simulations with sandbags, but, at the end of the day, you have to test things empirically."

ON TRAIN COMPANIES, STUPID ROUTINE EXCUSES BY, PART 1:

In another great moment from British Rail, Professor Sir Roland Smith complained about fleas in a sleeping car. He got a "personal" letter of apology from the chief of British Rail, Sir Bob Reid, along with an attached memo that said: "Send standard flea letter."

ON TRAIN COMPANIES, STUPID ROUTINE EXCUSES BY, PART 2:

In yet another great moment, a spokesman for British Rail explained the company's ultimate nondiscrimination attitude: "Would-be saboteurs have a perfect right to be on the platform, provided they have bought a ticket. It is not the job of our staff to arrest passengers carrying rocket-launchers. . . ."

ON TRAIN STATIONS, STUPID:

British Rail decided to build a roof canopy over the train platform at its train station in Penzance, England, to keep passengers out of the rain.

But they made the canopy a little too well. It not only kept the rain *out,* it kept all diesel fumes from the train engine *in.* People waiting for the trains coughed and hacked in the smoke-filled air. But never fear. Smart British Rail officials had a plan. . . .

As a spokesman said: "Arriving trains stop as normal inside the station. The engine is then shut down. A second engine is then attached to the rear of the arriving train. The engine tows the train out of the canopy to the new alighting–departing fume-free platform."

Of course, the "new alighting–departing fume-free platform" has no roof over it—and is open to rain, wind, and snow, just like the original platform before the "improvement."

ON TRAIN STATIONS, STUPID–RUNNER-UP:

Passengers waiting for the train at Hamble Station in England saw their train pull in—but instead of letting them on, they heard an announcement.

"You are not to board this train which has only stopped to let you know that it does not stop here on Sundays."

Unbelievably, the train then pulled out. A British Rail spokesman explained that this was an "economy measure" to save power. Passengers walked to the next station, where they were let on.

ON TRANSLATIONS, ENTHUSIASM FOR:

When governor of California, Ronald Reagan delivered a speech in Mexico City. He didn't speak Spanish, so he made his speech in English. Nevertheless, he was a bit disappointed by the tepid applause he received and more than a bit embarrassed—especially when the speaker who followed him, who was speaking in Spanish, was greeted with enthusiastic applause after each paragraph. To hide his embarrassment, Reagan joined in with the enthusiastic applause and, in fact, did the audience one better. He began clapping before anyone else did and continued clapping after everyone else stopped.

Then the U.S. ambassador leaned over. "I wouldn't do that if I were you," he said to the governor. "He's interpreting your speech."

ON TRANSLATORS, WHY WE PAY THEM:

Translators are supposed to translate from one language into another. But the translator at the press conference after the U.S.–Germany handball match didn't seem to realize this.

A reporter asked the U.S. coach, Javier Cuesta, how long his team had been training—in German. Cuesta replied—in English: "We've been together since January, training five days a week, four to five hours a day."

The translator then took the microphone and helpfully said—in English: "We've been together since January, training five days a week, four to five hours a day."

U

ON UMPIRES, GULLIBLE:

In the 1950s, American League umpire Jack Kerns had a reputation for never stopping a game early.

It could be pouring, it could be pitch black, but Kerns wouldn't declare the game over. As far as he was concerned, a baseball game should run nine innings or more—never less.

One late afternoon in Washington's Griffith Stadium, Kerns yet again was refusing to call the game and the desperate pitcher came up with an idea that he shared with his catcher. The batter already had two strikes on him. Instead of risking another pitch, the pitcher would wind up and *pretend* to throw the ball, while the catcher would keep the ball hidden in his mitt. After the pitcher had pretended to throw, the catcher would pop his mitt, as though he'd caught the ball.

And that's what they did. Apparently, it was convincing. Kerns didn't realize that there never had been an actual pitch.

"Strike three and out!" he yelled.

Apparently, the fake pitch was *very* convincing: The batter then turned to the umpire. "Strike? You blind son of a bitch! That ball was two feet outside!"

V

ON VACUUM CLEANER HISTORY, DECISIVE MOMENTS IN:

The inventor of the vacuum cleaner was a British gentleman named Hubert Cecil Booth. The almost-inventor of the vacuum cleaner was a brilliantly stupid American inventor who gave his idea to Booth.

What happened was this. Booth was visiting a London music hall in 1901 when he saw that one of the acts was an American who was demonstrating his carpet-dust-removing machine.

The machine was a box with a bag on top. It worked . . . sort of. The problem was that it *blew* the dust off the carpet. After the show, Booth went to the inventor. "It should suck, not blow," he said.

The American was furious. "Suck? Suck? Sucking is not possible," he said as he stormed past Booth.

W

ON WAITERS, BIZARRE:

A customer at a South Indian restaurant, celebrating her wedding anniversary with her husband, noticed a cockroach on the plate.

She called the waiter.

To her surprise, he picked up the roach and popped it in his mouth, saying, "This is a delicious onion, not a cockroach."

The waiter was shortly thereafter promoted to headwaiter. As the restaurant's owner enigmatically explained: "He is a man who may well give many years of good service."

ON WEAPONS, HOTSY-TOTSY:

The U.S. Army's Divad antiaircraft cannon was designed to be a weapon to be reckoned with. It was described by the Army in 1982 as "the most sophisticated piece of equipment ever to roll onto a battle-field."

Sophisticated, maybe. But there were, well, a few minor bugs.

First of all, the Divad didn't work too well in rain. And it didn't work very well at night, either. And sand tended to gum up its works.

In fairness, though, it *was* ideal for wars held in dry, sunny climates without dust, sand, mud, or darkness.

The Divad had other problems, too. It sent out a radar signal so strong that it was impossible to mask it, making it a sitting duck for the aircraft it was supposed to defend against.

But then again, the Divad's electronic aiming system couldn't aim well enough to shoot down the planes anyway. Tests revealed that human eyes worked better than the Divad. And if human eyes have difficulty in focusing on supersonic fighter jets coming in at twice the speed of sound, you can imagine the problems the Divad had. If, however, an enemy decided to launch any slow-flying Piper Cubs, the Divad was ideal . . . as long as it was daytime and it wasn't raining.

Of course, the Army refused to give up its baby. Instead, it held a public show to show the Divad at work. Unfortunately, on its debut, the Divad's computers malfunctioned. The computer made the cannon swing away from the target. Instead, it turned toward the reviewing stand—forcing all the generals and experts to duck fast for cover.

On second thought, though, they really shouldn't have bothered. The Divad probably would have missed.

ON WEATHERMEN:

In April of 1994, the newscaster on the main evening news show in New Delhi, India, made a startling announcement: "The weather has been canceled until further notice. It's all got too complicated to explain and we keep getting it wrong anyway."

It was a logical move, given the trouble the news station had been having.

Said a spokesman for the station in *The Times* of India the following Sunday: "It's been an abnormal April with, quite literally, scorching sunshine one minute and bitter winds and rain the next. On Monday evening, our weatherman told viewers, quite literally, to keep their woolen underwear on, and next day the temperature was 102. On Tuesday, he promised more sunshine, and we had four inches of snow. He's a professional meteorologist, and, when the death threats from viewers came in, he took it all very personally. He spent all Wednesday quite literally memorizing a long report, and tried to explain the freak conditions using satellite pictures, but, halfway through the evening broadcast, he forgot what he was talking about, and, quite literally, he couldn't go on. He just kept smiling nervously and adjusting his tie while repeating, 'If the snow cover over the Himalayas is sparse, it will surely lead to a good monsoon,' until he started to cry and eventually we quite literally faded him out.

"We haven't seen him since. We'll try him again next month, though. It's always blazing hot every day in May, so he should be able to cope. But I'm not sure he will return. His granny was attacked by an irate farmer with a chainsaw. Quite literally."

ON WHITE HOUSE CORRESPONDENCE, TASTEFUL:

Upset over the unemployment situation in 1981, a woman sat down and wrote a letter directly to President Ronald Reagan.

She waited for a reply, fully expecting a form letter spelling out Reagan's views on unemployment, any actions he had taken, and the like. And when a reply finally came, it was a form letter as she had expected. But it wasn't about unemployment. Instead, it gave her the Reagans' favorite recipe for crabmeat casserole.

Something had gone wrong, the woman informed the White House. Surely someone could rectify the situation and get her the information she wanted.

Word got to the President of the foul-up, and a *Newsweek* article mentioned that the letter had caused Reagan "considerable embarrassment."

So the system kicked in. The White House correspondence unit, which is responsible for screening mail and categorizing it for appropriate responses, got right on the matter. To avoid causing the President any further embarrassment, it immediately took action.

It pulled the crabmeat casserole recipe, replacing it with a more homey and down-to-earth macaroni and cheese.

ON WRESTLING, STRANGE MOMENTS IN:

Stanley Pinto was a professional wrestler who successfully faced a number of tough opponents—but during a match in Providence, Rhode Island, he lost to his most formidable opponent.

The bell rang, the opening minutes began ticking off, and Pinto found himself slightly entangled in the ropes. Eager to free himself, he began struggling wildly.

Before he could stop himself, he had pinned his own shoulders to the mat. His shoulders stayed pinned, despite his efforts to free himself. While his opponent—who hadn't laid a hand on him—watched, the referee began the countdown. And Pinto was counted out.

Y

On Yachting, Un-Yachtsmanlike Behavior and:

Seeing that a yacht off the coast of Brighton, England, had hoisted an emergency flag, Coast Guard officials rushed to send a helicopter and three lifeboats to the rescue.

When they boarded the boat in trouble, they found that they were on board with the world's worst yachtsman.

The first hint of this: He was navigating by means of an Automobile Association road map.

Even so, the intrepid yachtsman was unperturbed—and a little surprised that the Coast Guard had rushed to his rescue. There was no emergency, he explained. At least, not yet.

What about the emergency signals that had been hoisted?

His wife had gotten the pennants mixed up in the lunch basket.

The yachtsman's wife was not as calm. In her words, "I thought my husband was an experienced sailor, but when I looked at the [road] map and saw that the Isle of Wight appeared as a pinhead, I began to feel uneasy."

ON YELLOW STREETLIGHTS, LITTLE-KNOWN FACTS ABOUT:

The Bedford Gas and Light Company in 1979 announced plans to put in yellow streetlights at a town on Cape Cod.

But Lois Crane, a color consultant, launched an angry campaign against them. The reason? Yellow, combined with the red traffic lights, would incite people to wild sex.

But people were not convinced. What about some *proof,* some scientific *evidence* for this theory?

Crane was not deterred. She had proof.

"I once drove past a motel with amber lights in Washington. I wanted to scream, throw rocks, dance naked, and copulate—all at the same time. But I managed to restrain myself because I am seventy-three."